Analytic Group Consultation for Intermediate Beginners

Analytic Group Consultation for Intermediate Beginners provides a complete, accessible guide to running groups, and addresses the gaps in training and the challenges that emerge in the group therapy experience.

Presented in bite-size sections that follow the rhythm of weekly consultation sessions, the book offers an experienced perspective on facilitating groups, addressing specific questions, challenges, and dynamics that may emerge during the process. It begins with common issues in starting a group—introducing it, demystifying the experience, translating symptoms into therapeutic goals, and clarifying its value in complementing individual treatment. Byk outlines key theories that inform his work, including object relations theory, systems theory, and ego psychology, providing a solid theoretical foundation for purposeful interventions. The book explores working with depression, boredom, projective identification, scapegoating, role locks, flooding, and enactments, and addresses difficult dynamics such as the "elephant in the room," guilt, shame, and the power of witnessing repair in group settings. Providing a solid base for practitioners to work from, the book compellingly explains how group therapy can help patients, and how to communicate its benefits to them.

Analytic Group Consultation for Intermediate Beginners will be of great interest to psychoanalysts and mental health practitioners in training, and those starting in group therapy. It will also be of interest to academics and students of psychology, psychiatry, and social work.

Arthur C. Byk, LCSW, is a New York based, analytically oriented psychotherapist in private practice, focused on individual, group, and couples therapy. He has five therapy groups that have been meeting for over 35 years. In his career he has led more than 8,500 group therapy and group consultation sessions.

Analytic Group Consultation for Intermediate Beginners

What I Wish I Knew When I Started to Run Groups

Arthur C. Byk

Routledge
Taylor & Francis Group

LONDON AND NEW YORK

Designed cover image: Getty | LorenzoPatoia

First published 2026
by Routledge
4 Park Square, Milton Park, Abingdon, Oxon OX14 4RN

and by Routledge
605 Third Avenue, New York, NY 10158

Routledge is an imprint of the Taylor & Francis Group, an informa business

Author's Note: For reasons of confidentiality the names and other identifying
characteristics of all patients and consultees have been changed.

British Library Cataloguing-in-Publication Data
A catalogue record for this book is available from the British Library

ISBN: 978-1-041-09348-0 (hbk)
ISBN: 978-1-041-09347-3 (pbk)
ISBN: 978-1-003-64963-2 (ebk)

DOI: 10.4324/9781003649632

Typeset in Times New Roman
by Taylor & Francis Books

To Laura

Contents

About the Author

Arthur C. Byk, LCSW, is an analytically oriented psychotherapist in private practice in New York, offering individual, group, and couples therapy. He has five therapy groups that have been meeting for over 35 years.

In his career, he has led more than 8,500 group therapy sessions. His private consultation group has been meeting since 2002. He has taught group theory and practice, led process groups in postgraduate institutes, and supervised graduate students and psychiatry residents. He has presented workshops focused on group process at professional conferences.

Acknowledgments

This book is the outgrowth of over 40 years of learning, teaching, and facilitating group therapy. The idea for this work started as a suggestion by a former student, Simon Bresler, who accumulated over one hundred pages of notes taken in my classes. Another former student, Adi Avivi, joined us shortly afterwards. Simon and Adi were both instrumental in providing valuable structure and energy to the beginning stages of this work.

Over the years, I have had the good fortune to work with three practitioners whom I consider my mentors: Sydney Cohen provided me with the foundation of my work in psychotherapy and, most importantly, taught me "It's all grist for the mill"; Alan Shanel, whose open, reliable, and warm approach to therapy encouraged and challenged me to spread my wings; and Yvonne Agazarian, whose remarkable creativity and ability to integrate group-as-a-whole and systems theory provided me with oxygen to stimulate creativity in my own work.

I want to express my gratitude to Lee Kassan, who saw value in my manuscript and made it more cogent and coherent through his thoughtful editing. I would like to thank Earl Hopper for his reading and encouraging validation of the manuscript. I am also very grateful to Susannah Frearson at Routledge, who thought the work had potential and who, through her reliable and supportive guidance, opened up the path to publication. I want to also acknowledge my patients and consultees, who trusted me enough to make themselves vulnerable in our mutual effort.

Lastly, I want to thank my wife, Laura, who provided her love, support, encouragement, and time, which carried me through the hours of work that were so meaningful to me.

Preface

My Introduction to Group

My first experience with group therapy was as a patient. It was 1982, and my therapist, a well-regarded senior clinician, started one of my individual sessions saying, "I want you to start group therapy." He gave me no reason why. When I asked, he responded that it would enhance my therapy. Because I was in awe of my therapist, I complied. My experience was very interesting as well as intimidating.

I was given no instruction as to how to approach the group and no clarity as to what the goal was, other than vague reassurances that it would reinforce my therapy. At first, I convinced myself that I was using the group experience more to learn about being a group therapist in action, and less as a vehicle for self-awareness. Over time, I recognized how much I was learning about myself in the world. During the next several years, I had experiences in group that were actually life-changing.

My first lesson in self-awareness occurred a few months after I joined the group. A fellow group member, out of the blue, screamed at me, "You're so patronizing!" I asked her what she meant. "What did I do?" I couldn't really understand what I had done for her to be so upset with me. Others in the group agreed that I did seem patronizing but suggested that her reaction was extreme. I told the group that normally I would have dismissed her because of her extreme reaction.

I was embarrassed to admit that I didn't really understand what she meant by my being "patronizing." The group therapist asked if I would like my groupmates to point out if and when they felt patronized by me. I was puzzled but I was curious. I answered, "Sure." Privately, I felt stung, and wondered if this was the right group for me.

After the group meeting, I found my dictionary and looked up the word *patronizing*. I was surprised to see that synonyms included condescending, superior, pompous, and haughty. In no way did I experience myself that way. If anything, I felt intimidated, unsure, and vulnerable.

During the next session, I asked the group to point out when I was behaving in a patronizing way. To my great surprise, later in that same session, the same group member who screamed at me the previous session, in a loud voice, exclaimed,

"You're doing it right now."

"I'm doing what? What am I doing?"

"You're giving me advice. I already have a therapist. I didn't ask for your advice. I feel so patronized when you give me advice that I never asked for."

At that moment, I became aware that I was alienating some group members in being perceived as elevating myself by giving unsolicited advice. I thought I was doing a good thing. I thought that was what we should do. I thought I was being helpful and would be appreciated for that help. It was a familiar role I was encouraged to take on in my family.

I began to realize that often it was not appreciated at all. This awareness helped me, as I began to recognize how I was doing this in my outside life, frequently with the same unintended outcome. For the first time in my life, I was given the opportunity to become aware of my impact on others, without being exposed to a negative consequence other than feeling exposed and embarrassed. At least I didn't lose the relationship without a clue as to why. I never received this sort of feedback in my day-to-day life. And if I did, I probably would have dismissed it.

I stayed in group therapy for the next three and a half decades with several different practitioners. Gradually, I came to appreciate the power of the experience. I became more aware of how I was being perceived by others, regardless of my good intentions. I had the opportunity to practice recognizing when and why I went into my helper role. This was one among many learnings I was exposed to in my group experience.

My participation in group therapy, as well as my teaching of group theory and practice, has given me invaluable experience and knowledge that I have been able to incorporate into my practice of individual and group therapy. Presently, I have five relational/interpersonal therapy groups that have been meeting continuously for 35 years. I have a consultation group that has been meeting weekly since 2002. My experience has translated into having led over 8,500 therapy and process groups during this period.

Several years ago, I was approached by a former student, Simon Bresler, who enthusiastically suggested that it would be a worthwhile endeavor to write down my experiences participating in, leading, and teaching group therapy. Adi Avivi joined us shortly afterwards. Simon's and Adi's efforts were instrumental in the beginning stages of this book.

Introduction

As a consequence of my good fortune in teaching classes in group theory and practice, as well as in conducting consultations and consultation groups focused on group process, I have found that many group therapists were facilitating their therapy groups by utilizing a "grab bag" of techniques. Some practitioners reflected on their group experience as running their groups "by the seat of their pants." They didn't have a clear idea of the dynamics unfolding in front of them.

I noticed that certain issues would be brought up in consultation on a regular basis. Questions about how to introduce group therapy to patients, clarifying how group can be useful as an adjunct to their individual work, helping patients take in feedback without taking it personally, and not being able to recognize the difference between process and content were just the tip of the iceberg in their challenge to translate group into a useful therapeutic experience for their patients.

Presentations were lacking an awareness of the patient's goals. There seemed to be an emphasis on the "headline of the week." An emphasis on safety and not shaming their patients left therapists without a path to providing important feedback to their patients. There was frequent hesitancy to address the patient's contributions to the problems they were working on.

Many consultees reported that their groups, in some ways, were "dead in the water." Others reported that their groups were polite and avoidant. Interventions were intellectual and split off from emotion. There was a tendency for group members to analyze each other, with members taking turns sitting in the hot seat. There would be moments of great insight without it being translated to the here-and-now experience in the group. These groups, which at first had a great deal of energy, would, over time, become cautious and redundant.

My hope is that this book will be a useful tool for beginning practitioners who are just starting out, as well as experienced group therapists who find themselves in need of reinforcement of what they have already learned, as well as perhaps a new perspective. My central intention for the book is to clarify and facilitate the process of the group experience, which can serve as a pathway to discovering the patient's contribution to their problems or, as we say, their "nickel in the dime."

My approach in writing this book is to present over 125 sections, each addressing problems and/or issues that have come up in my consultation groups. I have attempted to infuse each section with the quality and feel of how I conduct my consultations in group therapy. Week after week we never know what is going to emerge in the group process. Content inevitably changes. Being familiar with theories of group and individual dynamics gives the practitioner the ability to see below the content, and to address the underlying dysfunctional roles, patterns of behavior, and barriers that undermine a patient's efforts to be effective in reaching their goals.

My objective in writing this book is to build upon the concepts of group theory and practice by addressing the actual experiences and challenges that we encounter in the group therapy session. The structure and format of the book attempt to mirror the group process, which, at first, can seem to be unstructured, disorganized, chaotic, and meandering, evolving into meaningful learning and discovery through thoughtful and informed interventions.

All case examples of the group process come directly from my therapy groups or group consultations. I have used composites of patients and issues to highlight the themes that are being presented. Identifying details of group members have been changed to ensure confidentiality and/or privacy.

Chapter 1

Beginnings

The Parable of the Long Spoons

When introducing the prospect of group therapy to a patient, I often ask if they are familiar with the parable of the long spoons. Usually, they are not. They ask me what that has to do with group therapy. I respond by sharing the version I am familiar with:

> Mr. Jones has died and finds himself at the gates of heaven. The gate-keeper welcomes him and informs him that, as a result of the life he has led, he is to be admitted to Heaven. The gatekeeper asks Mr. Jones to follow him. As they proceed, they eventually find themselves in front of two very large identical doors. The gatekeeper tells Mr. Jones that the first door is the door to Hell, the second is the door to Heaven. He asks Mr. Jones if he would like to see Hell before they enter Heaven. Always a bit cautious, Mr. Jones asks, "This isn't a trick, is it?" The gatekeeper reassures him that it is not. Jones agrees to take a look at Hell.
>
> Upon opening the door, Mr. Jones sees a dozen people sitting around a very large round table. In the center of the table is a massive bowl filled with a delicious-looking stew that fills the room with its wonderful aroma. As he looks more closely, he notices everyone looks wretched, despairing, miserable, and starving. They are moaning and sobbing.
>
> He realizes that each person has been given a very long spoon in order to reach the tempting stew that sits in the middle of the table. No matter how hard they try, because of the length of the spoon, each person finds it impossible to place the spoon and its contents in his or her mouth. It ends up on their clothes, on the floor, on the table—everywhere but their mouths.
>
> Jones continued to follow the gatekeeper out of the room, down the hall, and through the other identical door. Inside, he is surprised to see the identical set-up. There is a large table with a dozen people seated around it. There is a steaming fragrant stew in the middle of the table. Every person has an extra-long spoon to reach the stew.

DOI: 10.4324/9781003649632-1

At first, he is surprised to see everyone lighthearted, in good spirits, and well fed. What he notices a moment later is that instead of using the long spoons to feed themselves, they have found a way to deal with their dilemma by using the spoons to feed each other.

This solution, he realizes, is the difference between Heaven and Hell.

Demystifying the Group Experience

In contrast to my initial exposure to group, which is a common way of introducing a patient to group therapy, I try to demystify the group experience. I attempt to provide clarity as to why I am encouraging my patients to join a group and how it can help. This clarity seems to strengthen the therapeutic alliance and increase patients' motivation to learn about themselves, which frequently leads to a more successful therapeutic outcome (Rutan & Stone, 2001).

I find it productive to help the patient understand that group therapy is an opportunity to be exposed to and encounter experientially, not only intellectually, the way they contribute to the problems that brought them into treatment. This clarification seems to make the therapy experience more immediate and relatable to the patient (Ormont, 1992). Over the years, I have developed a reliable progression in my work that takes the same path for most patients.

First, I begin with individual treatment. Generally, within the first year, after spending time clarifying issues, themes, and goals, a therapeutic alliance (which I will discuss later) is usually established. At that point, I suggest group as an adjunct to individual therapy. I try to be unambiguous about why I am making this suggestion, keeping in mind the issues that the patient is presenting with. I attempt to clarify how group gives us a chance to translate experientially what we have worked on in the individual therapy. I introduce the prospect of a here-and-now environment that can help us witness what the patient can't observe in his reports of his outside life.

Over time, the group experience becomes the key to the patient's therapeutic learning. Individual treatment gradually begins to focus on the issues that emerge in the patient's group experience. Over time, the patient may drop weekly individual sessions, coming every other week. Many patients sustain their therapy by remaining in group and having one individual session a month. After several years, many patients report having increased success in moving toward their goals; they continue working in the group, and drop the individual sessions entirely.

Considerations in Starting a Group

Therapists who ask me about running groups report having been motivated by a variety of reasons. Some, having had their own experiences with group therapy, believe it could be helpful in their work with patients. Some conclude that their individual work was useful but not sufficient in helping their patients reach their goals. Some are motivated by the prospect of additional income. Some actually have no real clear reason for wanting to start a group but think they should because their own therapist ran groups.

I have found facilitating group therapy, in many ways, to be the glue of my practice.

Patients regularly report that the group experience reinforces their therapeutic learning. Having group members experience their growth and development with witnesses reinforces their enthusiasm for therapeutic work. Being able to struggle, fail, and succeed in view of witnesses who are not judging them contributes to patients taking more chances in attempting to reach their goals. Group therapy can contribute to the therapy experience coming alive and being less intellectual.

In terms of stabilizing a private practice, I have noticed that patients in groups are more likely to send referrals than patients in individual treatment alone. Groups can become a very reliable source of income. Having five to eight patients paying a moderate fee can frequently add up to a cumulative fee that is significantly higher than fees charged for individual sessions. My groups have been a financial bedrock of my practice for over 35 years.

How Group Can Add Value to Individual Treatment

Over the years, I have had many referrals when patients in individual therapy with other practitioners report that they "feel stuck" in their lives, and "stuck in their therapy." In addition, I have also been consulted by therapists who have reported feeling stuck in their work with patients. I have encountered patients who have become resigned to what they believe is unchangeable in them. They often believe that therapy, which initially seemed promising, cannot really help.

Group can help "unstick" patients by providing an environment where they can explore and experience themselves actually interacting in the interpersonal world. This experience is frequently in contrast to how they think they interact in the world. The therapeutic process involves identifying and exploring parts of patients that are invisible to them. They are not aware of how they may be contributing to the problems they are experiencing in their lives and coming into therapy to resolve (Yalom & Leszcz, 2005).

When patients in individual psychotherapy report their issues, we often risk establishing limited and sometimes distorted narratives of what is contributing to the problems that they are presenting with. The therapist may not be able to make sense of how patients are contributing to the presenting complaint solely from the reports of their life experiences or from the transference and/or countertransference that unfolds in session. The group experience can help expose the patient's idiosyncratic perspectives, patterns of behavior, and belief systems that may not be obvious or addressed in individual sessions.

How Group Can Free Up the Therapist

One common problem in individual treatment occurs when the therapist is reluctant to share his or her perspective with the patient because of over-whelming countertransference or transference reactions. Frequently, the therapist is not comfortable giving feedback to the patient out of a concern that the feedback will be experienced as critical.

I have seen delicate moments in group where patients were more available to feedback from their groupmates than from the therapist. Sometimes, difficult feedback presented by fellow group members gives the therapist some room to explore the patient's reactions to this feedback without being the source of what can be experienced as critical.

Introducing Group

A Common Problem

Stephen A., a psychologist, has been in private practice for seven years and has attended several group therapy trainings. He decides that he wants to start a group and begins mentioning it to some of his patients by saying, "I'd like you to join my group." In response to this idea, he is met with lukewarm interest and a host of ambivalence.

"I don't want to spend my time listening to other people's problems."

"I don't like people."

"How exactly is this going to help me?"

"I tried group therapy before, and it didn't help."

Realizing that he doesn't have an answer to his patients' valid questions and feeling disheartened, Stephen recognizes that it is important for him to become clearer with himself and his patients as to why he is starting this group and/or how his patients will benefit from the experience.

Clarifying How Group Can Help

I frequently give the example of someone who called me for a consultation.

Jill, 38, a successful software engineer, sought therapy to help in what she described as "tense" relationships with her husband and male boss. She had heard from a colleague that I was helpful in dealing with "relationship issues." Jill had been in two therapies, one analytic, the other CBT, lasting a year each. She reported that her therapists helped her understand that the problems she experienced with her husband and boss stemmed from issues related to her relationship with her loving but seemingly impotent father. Jill's father seemed to be her ally in fending off the judgments of her well-intentioned but unpredictably harsh mother.

She was told by her therapists that she identified with her depressed, resentful, and volatile mother. She was encouraged to practice "exercises" to calm herself down when she became "hot." She felt better during the therapy, but nothing changed in her relationships with husband or boss, or in relationship with herself. She left both therapists feeling hopeless about her problem but felt "supported" by both therapists.

Jill called me for a consultation after speaking to a friend who shared with her that I was helpful with several problems that seemed "hopeless." After several months of individual sessions, I suggested that she add group to her individual sessions. She was not happy about my proposal. She insisted that she was already feeling better coming to individual sessions. "I don't feel comfortable opening up my personal life to other people," she protested.

I told her that I believed the group would be a very important adjunct to our individual sessions. I explained to her how group works. She wasn't very impressed or interested, but she said she would give it a try since I thought it would help her therapy. She was giving me "the benefit of the doubt."

Jill joined a group composed of two straight women, two straight men, one gay man, and one gay woman. She seemed to fit in quite well. She developed alliances with the straight women and the gay members, who would engage her in support and mutual teasing. Her interactions with the straight men were polite and basically at arm's length.

After about six months of sessions, one of the straight men, Jack (who, coincidentally, was working on frustration tolerance and anger issues), seemingly out of the blue, yelled at Jill, "I can't take this anymore. Every time I open my mouth, you either change the subject, roll your eyes, or comment on how I don't get it. You are a bitch."

Several members were startled by the outburst, and focused on Jack's extreme reaction to what he perceived was hostility from Jill. After a few moments, I asked the group if anyone noticed Jill's behavior before Jack's outburst. Responses ranged from, "Jill was kind of cool to Jack's opening up" to "She never gives Jack a break."

I asked Jill if she was surprised by these responses. She responded, "Yes. I don't see how I could have anything to do with Jack's unbelievable behavior." I asked her who in the group she trusted most to give her feedback about what just happened. She responded, "I trust Dave to be fair." Dave responded in his typical teasing way, "Sweetheart, when it comes to Jack, you can certainly be a bitch."

Jill, even though uncomfortable hearing this feedback from Dave, tried to stay open to it. Others in the group let her know that they too noticed how she generally seemed impatient when Jack opened up in group. This would be noticeable since she would subtly roll her eyes, frequently change the subject, or move the attention away from Jack.

We explored Jill's experience in group during her next individual session. She admitted that she had a lot of unexpressed contempt for Jack. She didn't realize it was so obvious. In exploring the part of her that Jack activated, she recognized that she frequently feels that way with her husband, whom she viewed as "needy" whenever he expressed vulnerability. To a lesser extent, she saw that she would have a similar reaction to her boss, who was very successful but very disorganized under pressure.

I reminded her that members in the group mentioned some passive-aggressive behaviors that could possibly provoke her husband or her boss. "An important part of the group experience is remembering that there is what is called a *parallel process*. What we do in the group we tend to do in our outside lives." I suggested that she try to observe her reactions when she experienced judgmental feelings toward her husband—notice her behavior as well as her tone of voice. I encouraged her to take note of her "nickel in the dime," which may have played out in group with Jack and might be happening in relationship to her husband.

Jill came back next week with a mixture of embarrassment and excitement. She reported that she noticed how she would frequently roll her eyes at her husband. On these occasions, it would inevitably end up in an argument or the uncomfortable avoidance of a fight. She was quite surprised that there did seem to be a parallel happening in the group that reflected issues in her life.

This realization was the start of very fruitful explorations of how Jill projected her own vulnerability onto her husband and boss. She began to understand how her inability to tolerate her own vulnerability led to self-defeating and damaging consequences in relation to important dependency relationships. It was a significant turning point in her therapy that was greatly facilitated by her group experience.

We can understand this problematic situation as Jill containing the experience of "badness" in her feeling contempt for Jack's revealing his vulnerability. She projected the badness (her bad, uncomfortable feeling) into Jack by her behavior (rolling her eyes when he spoke, changing the subject, etc.). The induced badness (feeling judged, belittled, provoked) led to Jack's acting out (screaming at Jill), leaving him holding, containing the badness (and appearing "bad").

In Jill's subsequent explorations, she discovered that when Jack showed vulnerability it was a look-alike event for her. This experience provoked contempt for Jack, who became a stand-in for her "passive, useless father." Jack was also the current stand-in for her husband and her boss.

Recognizing how her experience with Jack was an echo of her relationship with her father and a mirror to what was happening in her current life was at first very upsetting. Jill's upset soon turned to curiosity, which developed into hope that maybe she could effect a change in the relationship with her husband.

Becoming aware of how it was her discomfort that led to her judging Jack and acting out by rolling her eyes, etc. led to her feeling true remorse for her behavior and initiating an active repair with Jack. Jill's experience in group translated into recognizing her "nickel in the dime," her part in the difficulties she was having with her husband and to a lesser extent with her boss.

This "snapshot" can provide opportunities to explore common role behaviors such as scapegoating (Jill scapegoating Jack), volunteering to be a scapegoat (Jack's behavior), projective identification leading to a role lock (victim/victimizer), and other issues we will discuss later.

Chapter 2

Theory That Has Informed My Group Perspective

I had the good fortune to teach individual and group theory at several analytic institutes for over 25 years. Having familiarity with theory has been indispensable to recognizing processes and formulating interventions that are purposeful and generally effective. Theory has helped me understand what I am seeing and experiencing in the group process instead of working intuitively and sometimes blindly. Over the years, I took pleasure in hearing from students that my manner of integrating and translating theory helped facilitate their understanding the dynamics of what they were presented with in group.

One example that stands out was a student reporting that, when he reframed what he viewed as a stubborn regression in a patient (which was developing into a battle of wills) as a reflection of Mahler's *rapprochement* (Mahler, Pine, & Bergman, 1975), he was able to use interventions that reflected this alternate perspective. He reported that this change in perspective freed him up to be more empathically attuned to his patient.

The following are authorities in the field whose theories have helped me in framing my thinking while leading groups. I am presenting my personal understanding of these theories and how I utilize them in facilitating group. I am not presenting these theories as an authority on these theorists. These are my personal interpretations of aspects of theory as I have understood them and have used them in facilitating group.

Wilfred Bion

Bion, as I understand him, suggested that group members regress and generally project intolerable experiences into the group (members) as a defense against unmanageable anxiety. The group "contains" the projections, leading to the formation of what he called *basic assumption* groups (Mitchell & Black, 1995). These are understood to be clusters of introjects that compel members to feel and act in specific ways. Members are attracted to and link with other members whose experiences are similar and create a recognizable valence of emotion in the group. He labeled these group-as-a-whole tendencies as "flight, fight, pairing, and dependency" basic assumption groups (Kibel, 1993).

DOI: 10.4324/9781003649632-2

It has been helpful to keep this in mind when the group as a whole is in:

Flight (continually avoiding conflict),

Fight (continued debating, talking over one another, taking feedback personally, yes-butting, etc.),

Pairing (an idealized pair of members seen as able to deal with challenges).

Dependency (never challenging the therapist, members never asserting their authority, staying passive, etc.).

It has been useful for me to think of the group as a container for the group members' experiences (Billow, 2000). I suggest to patients that the group *contains* group members' feelings and experiences as a bowl will contain soup. The function of containing is to hold (label, identify, frame) the experiences for the group members.

It has also been helpful to conceptualize each member as the container of experiences for the whole group. In one instance, Jill reveals that she feels sad. She doesn't know why. When we explore, we discover that her sadness reflects an unspoken sadness that several members in group acknowledge they are feeling after it is named.

Melanie Klein

Klein, as I understand her, proposed that the infant experiences ego development in two stages that she called the *paranoid/schizoid position* and the *depressive position*. These positions reflect fundamental ways of viewing the world (Kibel, 1993)

Paranoid/Schizoid Position

The *schizoid* side: very early on, the infant seems to relate to the mother (caretaker) through a prism of unrealistic merger and fusion. There is no experience of me/not me.

The *paranoid* side: soon the infant experiences unpleasant feelings of separateness. She doesn't get the milk (provisions) on demand and experiences frustration. The infant doesn't have the capacity to experience the existence of alternate states of feeling good and bad at the same time.

This leads to *splitting*. The infant flips back and forth between loving and hateful experiences of the environment. She experiences two mothers, one good, one bad. When she gets the milk (provisions), she experiences *idealization* of the object (mother) and *omnipotence*. When she doesn't get the provisions (milk, holding, etc.), she experiences *devaluation* of the object and *feelings of persecution*.

Splitting is understood to be the result of the infant not being able to tolerate ambivalence. We frequently see this tendency in our patients during the here-and-now experience of the group process. The infant can't remember the good when he is feeling bad, or feeling bad when he is feeling good.

What are examples of the paranoid/schizoid position in group? The tendency for members to avoid criticism by not revealing themselves, laying low, scapegoating each other (projecting out their badness into a groupmate or the group as a whole, etc.).

Depressive Position

In the *depressive* position (not depression), eventually the infant realizes that the withholding bad mother whom they hated is the same person as the good, providing mother whom they loved. The infant is now filled with concern that as a result of its hateful tendencies and greed the goodness of the mother has been contaminated or destroyed.

What are examples of the depressive position? Concern about being too critical of others, fear of hurting others, remorse for having injured a group-mate, etc. This developmental milestone results in the infant's experiencing sorrow, concern, and remorse, which in turn leads to the child's development of the capacity for concern.

How is knowing this theory helpful in group practice? The infant's/group member's growing ability to tolerate ambivalence and recognize its own hateful inclinations leads to:

Growth in reality testing;

Enhanced recognition of the availability of love and its limitations;

Aiding in the infant's/group member's capacity to tolerate frustration and disappointment;

Setting into motion an increased capacity to love.

The challenges and achievements of the infant echo and reflect the intrapsychic struggles that the adult is faced with when unable to tolerate frustration, discomfort, and disappointment in current life experience. The solution is to resort to splitting in order to maintain emotional stability. Awareness of this process translates readily into having a template for recognizing and working through the dynamics that contribute to polarized moments occurring in the group process. Group members, under stress, frequently split their relationships into good and bad. Highlighting how group members are making their groupmates all good or all bad during difficult moments can help them realize how readily they can split their perceptions of the world, of other people, and of themselves.

I frame for the group how, as a result of integrating the split, remorse leading to the development of the *capacity for concern* is a critical developmental achievement in experiencing themselves realistically. When members experience repair in formerly polarized relationships that were distorted as a result of the tendency to split, it frequently leads to the experiences just outlined above (growth in reality testing, an enhanced ability to recognize the availability of love and its limitations, etc.). Many patients begin to notice, regretfully, how their tendency to split may have contributed to the difficulties in intimate relationships that brought them to therapy in the first place.

Otto Kernberg

Kernberg, as a result of his focus on behavior, translated Klein's abstractions into more therapeutically accessible premises. *Projection* and *projective identification* can be understood to be the motivations behind many of the provocative behaviors we witness in the group process (Greenberg & Mitchell, 1983; Kibel, 1993).

A simple way to recognize and understand the difference between *projection* and *projective identification* is that the target of the projection is not provoked by the behavior. In projective identification, the targeted individual is provoked by the behavior and gives the projection a "mate" (e.g., the mother becoming angry in reaction to the child's tantrum).

In projective identification, the child projects out his/her "badness" (bad feeling) into the mother behaviorally. The child throws a tantrum. The mother, reacting to the projection (in the form of the tantrum), is provoked, gets annoyed, angry, even furious, and gives a home to the child's anger. She is now *containing* the badness. The mother punishes the child and becomes the "bad mother."

Being able to recognize these processes can be very helpful in understanding and working with the dynamics related to the splitting and repair that is a bedrock of learning in our groups. Sooner or later, the child realizes that the good mother who provided the provisions is actually the same mother who withheld those provisions. This development, identified by the experience of sorrow, concern, and remorse, leads to the establishment of capacity for concern.

Reaching this developmental milestone is a critical achievement for many patients who tend to secure and isolate themselves in their anxiety by splitting. I have many patients who report that witnessing rupture and repair in group was one of their most profound learning experiences. They would report that they never saw repairs occur in their families or in significant relationships. Witnessing a relationship's rupture and its repair can contribute greatly to a group's cohesion. Patients are more likely to take chances in group. They know that if they happen to upset others there is a path to repairing the breach.

D. W. Winnicott

Several themes stand out in Winnicott's work in relation to group (Kibel, 1993). Winnicott focused on the mother–child relationship, where, he suggests, the child attaches to a *transitional object* (Mitchell & Black, 1995). This is understood to be the symbolic representation of the mother–child bond. The transitional object is an object that tends to have the smell of both the mother (caretaker) and the child intermingled. This transitional object, frequently taking the form of a security blanket, is embraced by the child as he or she separates from the mother and goes into the world. I was trained to view the group as a transitional object in the group member's life. One of the central goals of the group experience is to have members internalize and integrate their group learning and experience in order to utilize them in their outside lives.

Winnicott focused on the importance of available nurturing and supportive caretaking that provides the child with *good-enough mothering*. This experience provides the child with what Winnicott described as a *holding environment*. I understand the group to be a holding environment for group members. Good-enough mothering is an important concept for us as group facilitators, as well as for group members. There is often a tendency toward perfectionistic striving. I hold onto the theme that we should aim to be "good enough" (not aiming low or too high). I continually reinforce this notion in group.

I also keep in mind what Winnicott described as a *false self* vs. *true self* experience. The false self, being an adaptation to the child's challenging environment, is an emotional split from the underlying authentic experience; it is actually experienced to be true. The patient actually believes that they are inherently shy, stupid, uninteresting, deficient, etc. It is ego-syntonic.

Group can help patients recognize that they developed these false-self roles as a solution to the challenges they faced in their family environment. These false-self traits are frequently believed by the patient to be part of their character, inborn and unchangeable. I was trained to understand *character* to be patterns of behavior that endure over time. Group provides a holding environment for characterological change.

Margaret Mahler

As I understand her, Mahler describes a process of emotional growth and development in which the child progresses from a merged, symbiotic state, characterized by a lack of differentiation with the mother, through gradual experiences of separation/individuation (Mahler, Pine, & Bergman, 1975). What I first keep in mind is the stage of *practicing* (ages 10–14 months). The child develops from being prone, to crawling, to having the ability to perambulate. The world is her oyster.

During this period of development, the child's physical prowess bypasses his or her intellectual awareness of the challenges, frustrations, and difficulties in the world. Gradually, the child recognizes that the world is unpredictable, and they can get hurt. The child begins to regress back to a more cautious state, looking for more comfort and reassurance from the mother.

Mahler called this stage *rapprochement*. Rapprochement is a very significant developmental stage in which the child needs to be reassured and then encouraged to go back into the world and explore. Some caregivers aren't attuned and do not recognize the child's need for holding and reassurance. This type of caregiver sends the child out into the world prematurely, without adequate emotional supplies. This experience can lead the child to become increasingly clingy. This lack of attunement may over time evolve into fears of abandonment in the adult.

At the other end of the continuum, fears of engulfment may develop as an outgrowth of the caregiver's loneliness, depression, etc. The caregiver delights in and encourages the child's increased clinginess. This child, without the necessary emotional supplies, may separate out prematurely. He or she intuitively pulls away from the clinginess of the caregiver. This can lead to the child growing into an adult who keeps dependency relationships at arm's length.

We frequently see the residue of fears of dependency in group. Members sometimes actually articulate it: "I don't need anyone." "I am a rock; I am an island." I point out that there is no way to not depend. We can experience healthy dependency, or unhealthy dependency. The group experience can facilitate differentiation between the two. Individuals who experienced inconsistent, undermining, and chaotic dependency relationships in childhood frequently convince themselves that they can live without depending on anyone.

I suggest that this is understood to be *pseudo-self-sufficiency*. We can live without attachments but cannot thrive (which is directly related to the presenting complaints of generalized anxiety, depression, problems in relationships, etc.).

René Spitz

When exploring fears of dependency, I often refer to René Spitz, whose work on infant growth and development focused on the importance of the mother–child relationship. When fears of dependency emerge in the group process, I may bring up the following account.

Spitz, a psychoanalyst, was consulted by a foundling hospital that had a ward of orphaned infants whose parents were killed during World War II. The infants were not developing normally. Even though these infants were otherwise well taken care of, Spitz observed that they were not, in general, physically held or emotionally related to. The resulting outcome for these infants was stunted development in height, weight, emotions, affect, etc. This developmental outcome was labeled a *failure to thrive*. He called this an *anaclitic depression*.

(Mitchell & Black, 1995)

Spitz recommended that the infants be held regularly, in addition to normal care. This seemingly obvious solution wasn't so obvious then. The infants, after being held and being more engaged by their caregivers, gradually resumed more normal growth and developmental patterns. His work added to the recognition of the basic need for attachment in human beings.

Yvonne Agazarian

I had the good fortune to study with Yvonne Agazarian for 15 years. Her theory, which she developed as the basis of System Centered Therapy (SCT), has been very influential in my understanding of group processes. I have used parts of her theories that fit well with my way of working. The following is my understanding of concepts that I have found very useful in facilitating groups.

"Systems are energy organizing ... goal directed ... self-correcting ... change and transform by integrating differences" (Agazarian, 1997, pp. 19–20). I try to keep in mind that I am working with the psychological system of the group member as well as the group as a whole.

Part of our work is to help the patient develop a more resilient internal emotional core in which they are able to discriminate and integrate differences more readily. Patients need differences to develop and grow, but they are frequently threatened by these same differences. The differences that patients have difficulty with are generally related to long-held perceptions of themselves and their environment.

I have found the process of integrating differences to be central to our work in helping patients reach their goals. As I understand Agazarian, if a patient has difficulty being open to exploring differences, we can understand their system to be in a shaky, unstable state. She described this internal state as *survival*. Differences are rejected out of hand. They are too threatening for this patient's system.

A solution to this problem is incorporating Agazarian's recommendation of introducing differences that are not too different. This work focuses on identifying and working through cognitive distortions and dysfunctional roles that contribute to destabilizing the patient. These distortions range from engaging in negative and positive predictions, projections in the form of mindreading, ruminations about the past, fears of the future. These cognitive distortions often give rise to an experience of unsafety and threat. Dysfunctional roles that were once functional are activated by these perceived threats and now ironically play a part in undermining the patient.

This perspective has been helpful to me in becoming more aware of and empathically attuned to the patient's resistance as being part of an emotional security system. Previously, my experience with resistance led me to understand it as an experience that was too difficult for the patient to tolerate. I was taught to try to "thin out" the resistance, not try to break through or confront the resistance as had been common in classical analysis. The problem was how to thin out the resistance.

Agazarian's suggestion of "introducing a difference that is not too different" (p. 19) has helped, in a practical way, frame my interventions in a manner that the patient is more likely to tolerate. This approach is in keeping with the perspective of thinning out, not confronting resistance. It has become a valuable tool in my therapeutic toolbox.

For example, I might say, "I think I see something that you may not see. Are you open to hearing it? I have a hunch that ... .". I then follow this intervention with an observation that is "not too different" from the patient's experience. In response to a patient's complaint that his wife was impossible to please, I suggested, "I think that in your excitement to do something special for your wife, you may not have paid attention to what she really wanted and missed the mark. What do you think?"

Agazarian developed a method of working in groups she referred to as *functional subgrouping*. She suggested that subgroups naturally develop around stereotypical similarities. She would deliberately encourage different subgroups to develop through the exploration of members' similar experiences. Eventually different subgroups would find similarities in listening to the explorations of the other subgroup. This process would typically lead to increased understanding and discovery of mutual experiences by the members in differing antagonistic or incompatible subgroups.

Periodically, I have used variations of Agazarian's technique. The technique I'm about to describe also has aspects of Harville Hendrix's methodology (Hendrix, 2007). When the group seems to lose energy or is on the verge of deepening explorations but keeps going back to explaining and intellectualization, I suggest to the group that I want them to try an effectiveness exercise or communication game. I suggest that this is an exercise in listening and communicating effectively.

I ask a member to say what is meaningful to them in a succinct manner so that someone else can remember what was said and be able to repeat it. I then have another group member repeat what was just introduced by the previous member. The last member has to repeat what the original member said until that first group member suggests that the second one got it. *Got it* means getting the sentiment of what the previous member was attempting to communicate. Once they get it, they are asked to build on the theme of what was revealed by the previous member, as it relates to them.

As group members attempt this exercise, they frequently learn that they are not listening carefully, as well as not communicating as effectively as they think they are. They begin to realize how difficult it is for them to "truly listen." They become aware of how difficult it is for them to build on what the last person said.

Members discover that they are going on too long and explaining too much. They begin to recognize how redundant and ineffective they can be in their communication. They realize how their interactions with others are filled with emotional *non sequiturs* and avoidance. They are frequently surprised to find that they were not listening carefully. They realize that this pattern occurs in their attempts at communicating outside of the group.

This exercise is not easy. As challenging as this exercise is, it can be very helpful in the here-and-now experience of the group. Patients learn how ineffective they can be in communicating and listening to others in their lives. They are often surprised by how challenging it is to stay focused, listen carefully, and respond succinctly. They become aware of how they were taking their efforts at communication for granted, never giving a thought to whether or not they were communicating effectively.

This exercise is not popular with most of my patients. There is, not infrequently, a group groan when I bring up the exercise or the game. Sometimes they see it as punishment. In exploring the resistance to this group exercise, members often admit that they are forced to accept and face limitations in their ability to communicate effectively. They struggle to admit to themselves that perhaps their limitations in communicating may be contributing to the problems they are complaining about. Patients frequently report that when they become more proficient and use this method in their lives, this simple and challenging skill increases their self-confidence in relating to others.

Chapter 3

Things to Keep in Mind When Introducing Group

When I suggest adding group to a patient's therapy, I keep in mind the *goals* of the individual and the *purpose* of the group format (Rutan & Stone, 2001). I introduce the perspective that the group format provides an opportunity for us to see how we actually relate to the world, not only how we think we relate to the world. By observing our interactions with others in the group environment, we have the chance to understand our strengths as well as the barriers that interfere with our developing the experiences and relationships we want to have.

I present to the patient the view that symptoms such as depression, generalized anxiety, isolation, poor impulse control, etc. can be addressed in group, since these symptoms, in one way or another, stem from feeling ineffective in the interpersonal world. Feeling ineffective leads to experiencing a lack of mastery, as well as shame and embarrassment, which can ultimately result in shaky self-esteem. The group format facilitates our discovering, experiencing, and working through what is contributing to our inability to be effective in our lives. These discoveries include recognizing and identifying projections, cognitive distortions, negative and positive predictions, and dysfunctional roles, as well as interpersonal deficits.

It is at this point that I clarify how I understand the concept of *self-esteem*, which is essential in our work.

Translating Symptoms, Presenting Problems, and Complaints into Therapeutic Goals

I believe an important undertaking for us is to translate symptoms and presenting complaints into practical goals. I find that patients' comprehension of how their complaints can be directly related to their experience and how they actually contribute to those complaints can give us leverage when resistance inevitably emerges. It makes the therapy less mysterious and more accessible to the patient.

Early on in treatment I introduce the therapeutic goal of recognizing our strengths, as well as clarifying what conflicts and deficits interfere with our effectiveness in moving toward goals centered on love and work. As I

DOI: 10.4324/9781003649632-3

mentioned earlier, my assumption is that our lack of effectiveness in our interpersonal world leads to many of the symptoms that patients present with. A common example is feeling "depressed."

> "So if I'm getting this right, you're telling me that your depression stops you from having the kind of relationships that you want because you lose energy and motivation, and start to feel hopeless about your future. This impacts your ability to go out into the world, engage with others in a fulfilling way, and to have hope for the future. Did I understand that correctly?"

In response, I reframe depression not as the *cause* of their feelings of hopelessness and helplessness, but as being the result of experiencing hopelessness, help-lessness, and low self-esteem due to a lack of mastery. I suggest that self-esteem is directly correlated to mastery. A lack of mastery in the interpersonal world results in low self-esteem and its derivative symptoms (depression, isolation, obsessions, compulsions, self-hatred, lack of energy, etc.). I propose that our work in therapy is to become more effective in mastering our interpersonal and work experiences. Becoming more effective leads to an increased sense of mastery, resulting in increased self-esteem, which is the underlying goal of our therapy.

This therapeutic process is accomplished in the group by experiencing, witnessing, and working through, in the here and now, the emotional conflicts and deficits that undermine the patient's interpersonal experience.

Differentiating Self-Esteem from Self-Image

Self-esteem, as I use the concept, is directly correlated to achieving mastery and feeling effective in the world as a result of mastery. I find this simple perspective translates easily into the patient's group experience.

Self-image, as I understand the term, is related to how I present the image of myself to the world. It is very possible to have the experience of having an ele-vated self-image (I'm strong, I'm beautiful, I'm clever, etc.) while having low self-esteem (I'm a fraud, I'm unlovable, I'm a failure, etc.). I have found that differ-entiating between the two in this simple manner gives patients a clearer emo-tional understanding of how their self-esteem is related to mastery of the internal (e.g., learning how to self-regulate) and interpersonal challenges they are pre-sented with in group. The group experience, if handled well, can address the experiences that contribute to challenges to the patient's self-esteem.

Character: Patterns of Behavior that Endure Over Time

Patients regularly suggest that their problems stem from their character or personality and cannot be changed. Patients often state, "I'm an angry (depressed, unlikeable, rageful, etc.) person. That's who I am." In response, I have found it useful to state that I understand *character* to reflect *patterns of behavior that endure over time.* I suggest to patients that these patterns of behavior are basically adaptations we formed in response to the family/social environment we were faced with in our growth and development.

The group experience gives us an opportunity to observe these patterns of behavior in vivo. It can help us understand how and why we developed these patterns and how we have imported them into our current lives. Group therapy can give us the opportunity to help patients recognize these patterns, learn their purpose, and choose, if they desire, to work on changing patterns that are maladaptive and undermining in their current lives.

Patients are generally relieved to have character understood in this way. It seems to neutralize a great deal of self-judgment that patients are burdened by when believing that their character is something that is immutable and inborn.

Chapter 4

A General Approach to Facilitating Group

In this section, I will try to integrate processes I have described in previous sections. My framework in facilitating groups has been to organize my observations and thinking as a function of the following processes:

1 Keeping in mind the patient's presenting complaints, which can be frequently forgotten in the airing of "headline" issues of the week.
2 Developing mutual assumptions that emerge from observations of the patient's behavior in group. These assumptions focus on the way members defend and stabilize themselves in response to challenging moments in the group process. These assumptions have to be agreed upon by both the patient and me; otherwise, they are not mutual. The establishment of mutual assumptions in relationship to the patient's presenting complaints leads us to:
3 The understanding of a patient's role behavior in group, which inevitably contributes to:
4 Discovering their "nickel in the dime" (understanding the patient's contribution to their presenting issues), which facilitates:
5 Having an opportunity to understand their experience from a larger perspective. One major goal is to develop the capacity to become "larger than the moment." Group members begin to recognize how their perspective and resulting behaviors affect their relationships in group as well as their relationships outside of group, which we identify as a parallel process. This gives the patient the opportunity to:
6 Use this knowledge in the service of giving them a choice.

Continuing to Do What They Do or Trying Something Different

When an authority issue emerges, it generally takes on recognizable forms such as a battle of wills, passive-aggressive behavior, taking on a victim position, fighting, arguing, debating, etc.

DOI: 10.4324/9781003649632-4

Richard, age 39, a high-level manager at a tech startup, was in therapy to work on difficulties with his wife and feeling threatened by negative evaluations from his reports at work.

During group sessions, I would periodically find myself engaged in heated debate with Richard. I would, after a few minutes, wonder, "How did we get here?" The debate inevitably took on the following pattern, which led to potentially polarized, uncomfortable moments.

Richard would, with a dismissive tone, challenge something I was saying. As always, I would give him plenty of space to make his point and ask him for his experience below whatever he was saying. Ignoring my suggestion to explore his experience, he would insist on a particular point, even if it didn't correspond or relate to what was being said. He would focus on the content and not appreciate the spirit of what was being explored. He wouldn't, or couldn't, as a groupmate suggested, "let go of the bone."

Eventually, I (or one of his groupmates) would try to clarify the spirit or essence of what was being said. The ensuing process would end up with his debating the groupmate or again debating me. His groupmates would ask him why he was debating. Why not be curious about what is being said? "I'm not debating!" he would argue. "Arthur is not making sense."

Upon exploring why he was getting so agitated and antagonistic, even if Arthur was not making any sense, he began to recognize that this was a common pattern that occurred with his wife, as well as in work relationships. He was open to reflecting on whether this was a "look-alike event" in his life.

He claimed that he wasn't debating. He was trying to "reason" with his wife, as he was trying to reason with me, his therapist. "I try to reason with both of you when you're not on the right track," he said. I asked him why it was so important to him that we be on the right track. He responded without hesitation, "I depend on you."

We discovered that these episodes were a recapitulation of common anxiety-inducing experiences Richard had as a child. Richard would debate his father when he perceived his "loving, well-intentioned father" being overwhelmed and ineffective with a perspective he believed left himself and his family vulnerable to the very challenging events they were faced with.

Richard wanted to convince his father that his perspective was "on the wrong track." He couldn't understand why his father wouldn't do or say anything about the situation the family was in. His debates didn't change anything in relation to the family situation, but they did leave him feeling some vague sense of power. At least he had said something.

We established a *mutual assumption* that when he started to debate me it was an indication that he was feeling vulnerable in trusting what I was saying. In his mind, if he went along with what I was saying and it was incorrect, it could lead to very bad outcomes, as had occurred in his family of origin.

He admitted that he depended on me and if I wasn't "on the right track" he felt upset, angry, and threatened. He was projecting his experience with his well-meaning but ineffective father onto me. We considered this constellation of thoughts, feelings, and behaviors to be a dysfunctional role that he labeled his *debate role.*

His goal in this role was to rescue his family and preserve himself. The role behavior was currently dysfunctional as it inevitably led to arguing and polarizing the relationship. The vague sense of power he felt as a child who stood up for himself was now ironically leading him to an experience of anxiety and powerlessness.

In group, I suggested to Richard that I wasn't invested in being right. If I was saying something that didn't make sense to him, would he consider staying curious about what I was saying instead of debating me? Could he simply state what he thought about what I or others were saying instead of debating and trying to convince us that we were wrong?

Whenever Richard started to debate me in group, I would ask him what he felt toward me at that moment. He would generally smile and say, "Am I debating you again? I guess I don't trust what you are saying."

We identified his fear of dependency in relation to authority. This issue occurred either when he was in a position of authority having to depend on subordinates, or when finding himself dependent on an authority figure. The group experience helped him recognize when he was going into his Debate Role. He learned to pause and reflect on his internal experience.

We helped him identify an early warning sign indicating that he was entering the role. The signal was a harsh, judgmental tone to his voice. He would, in his mind, elevate himself and judge the person he was relating to. He would then try to convince them that they were wrong. He would argue his case, which generally reflected the content of what was being said but not the sentiment. His tone of voice would inevitably betray his judgment, which would then antagonize the person he was debating. Below the judgment he experienced a sense of threat.

This dysfunctional role was now recognized as contributing to problems in relationship with his wife. This occurred when he had a different opinion about important family matters (i.e., where to send his son to school, moving to the suburbs, going on vacation, etc.). Instead of having an exchange of ideas, and being open to his wife's opinion, these discussions generally devolved into very unpleasant debates.

He gradually learned to recognize, identify, and express his fears or concerns rather than debate the merits of his wife's opinions, which would inevitably leave her feeling demeaned, pushed away, and angry at him. Richard reported, over time, appreciation for the insight and understanding that was facilitated in the group experience. He began to notice how and when he would start to debate with his wife. He recognized how his tone of voice could be experienced as demeaning. Over time he was happy to report that the relationship with his wife became less strained and more satisfying. He graciously attributed the change to what he learned about himself in group.

He also reported that his relationships at work, with his reports as well as his bosses, seemed to be less polarized. He began to notice how and when he would engage in debates with them. He recognized and paid attention to how his tone of voice could be experienced as very off-putting. Richard reported that the parts of his work evaluations focused on interpersonal effectiveness improved dramatically.

Engaging Role Locks

When there is an enactment in group, my assumption is that a *role lock* (Agazarian, 1997), a heightened emotional moment related to dependency, authority, fight, a look-alike event, etc., has materialized. The above section describes a role lock I would tend to enter into with my patient Richard. In this section, I elaborate on how I approach this challenging situation.

Working through an Authority Role Lock

1   Frequently, the initial signal is noticing heightened affect in myself, a group member, or the group as a whole.
2   I explore what is being induced in me (I am annoyed, frustrated, feeling impotent, feeling useless, etc.). Familiarity with and awareness of countertransference can be a useful tool in staying separate and not being induced into a role lock.

I find it helpful to differentiate between two types of countertransference conceptualized by Racker (outlined by Tansey & Burke, 1989). The experience in both types of countertransference is that I am experiencing heightened feelings that divert me away from my normal posture of staying separate, centered, and curious about the patient's experience.

> *Concordant Countertransference*: feeling similarly to what the patient is feeling.
> I may be feeling anxious, confused, overwhelmed, frustrated, upset, vulnerable, intimidated, etc. within myself in relation to the patient. The question I ask myself is, "Why am I feeling anxious, overwhelmed, and upset in dealing with Richard?"
> *Complementary Countertransference*: feeling similarly to what the other person in relationship to the patient could or would be feeling toward the patient.
> I may be feeling impotent, hostile, punishing, impatient, fed up, etc. with the patient. The question I ask myself is, "Why am I feeling punishing, impatient, impotent with Richard?"

3   I attempt to recognize and understand how I may be in a role lock with this particular patient. I examine how I may be contributing to it. I keep in mind how this may be characterological for the patient by remembering their history, dynamics, goals, and presenting complaints. I keep in mind my own subjective countertransference and emotional proclivities in this type of situation. I have learned that I have a tendency to slip into battles of will myself. I try to remember the patient's presenting complaints and goals in their therapy and how it may be playing out in the here-and-now experience of the group.

4   I "let go of the bone." In these intense moments I attempt to stay curious, take an emotional step back, and make an effort to be larger than the moment, which is not always easy to do. I might say "Okay, you win." This frequently results in the patient moving out of the charged emotional moment. "What do you mean, I win?" I generally respond with a variation of, "Whatever I think or say is less important in this moment than my understanding of what you are experiencing right now."

5   I re-establish our therapeutic alliance by asking,

ARTHUR: "How much do you trust me right now? 5, 10, 20%?"
PATIENT: "Maybe 5%."
ARTHUR: "Okay, can we examine what's going on between us using only that 5%?"

6   I suggest that this is a pattern that I have noticed. "Are you open to seeing what I see?"

7   I gently present what I think I see, based on their family history, presenting complaints, and the here-and-now experience of the group. If they are open to my "hunch" as to what might be going on, we can develop mutual assumptions about:

(A)   Their behavior in the here and now of the group experience, which might be contributing to the polarized situation they are experiencing.

(B)   How this behavior was a solution to problems faced in the family of origin. This is understood to be their role in the family.

(C)   How these behaviors/solutions were *functional* in dealing with the problems they faced in their family of origin.

However, in Richard's case, his tendency to debate, fight, become passive-aggressive, etc. are contributing to polarizing the relationships he is presently in. These solutions, which were once functional, are being imported into his current life and are now dysfunctional.

(D)   How this mutual assumption is directly related to his presenting complaints and the problems he is facing in his outside life. These problems commonly include difficulties in significant dependency relationships, feelings of isolation, not feeling connected to those closest to them, depression, etc.

In Richard's case, our mutual assumption centered on recognizing that he would tend to argue or debate when feeling vulnerable in a dependency relationship. This occurred when he was dependent on someone or in a position of authority where someone depended on him.

8   I give the patient a choice. I suggest to the patient that they now have a choice that they didn't have before. They can continue doing what they always do or use this new perspective to change their way of relating and see what happens.

9   When they defend against change: sometimes the patient responds with "I already tried this" or "What about the responsibility of the other person in this situation?" These responses are recognized in patients who instinctively reject help. They are a characteristic of patients who are known in the field as *help-rejecting complainers* (Yalom & Leszcz, 2005). I reply that, in general, when a person tries to change an entrenched family system it takes many attempts and patience to effect the system. As Agazarian (1997) suggested, systems do not like differences. We are introducing a difference. What's important is to introduce differences that are not too different. We have to be patient as the system attempts to integrate the difference.

> ARTHUR: "Yes, I understand you tried this before, however, you never tried it while working with me. Will you give it another try?"
> ARTHUR: "Yes, of course the other person is responsible as well. However, you're the only one here working on the situation. We can't change them. What we could try to do is change the system by changing the way you relate to them and seeing if it makes a difference."
> ARTHUR: "We have the choice of continuing to believe what we believe, act in the way we generally act, or trying to be open to a different perspective and behave accordingly, which may change (over time) an entrenched emotional system."

Chapter 5

General Considerations in Facilitating Group

The Support Trap

On occasion, patients will complain that they don't feel supported by me. This generally occurs when they don't feel comfortable with what I am presenting to them about themselves. Frequently, these patients have come into my practice after having experienced a stalemate in their previous therapy.

The patient will comment on how supportive the previous therapist was. I respond by reminding them that they decided to leave their previous therapist for some reason, and we should, of course, explore that reason. I do this to learn what went wrong in the previous therapy and to help them understand that we want to avoid that same experience here.

Often the exploration reveals that they felt very supported by their therapist but weren't making much progress in their life. The therapist's support felt very encouraging in the beginning. After a while, the support felt empty and redundant.

Not infrequently patients would report feeling "bound" to the therapist, who was the one person in their lives they felt safe with and supported by "no matter what I did or said." They would reveal that they had trouble leaving the previous therapist and felt "trapped" because they were always "so supportive" and "so nice." They would report that they didn't want to hurt the therapist.

Occasionally, these patients would leave abortively, without explanation. Others would take advantage of some "convenient" reason related to time or money. "I couldn't tell him that I wanted to leave therapy." I suggest to the patient that I wouldn't want us to get into the same predicament they were in with their last therapist.

I want them to understand that support in our work basically emerges from recognizing that we are in a collaboration, attempting to see what is stopping them from reaching their goals. It is not easy to look at what we are doing that is undermining our efforts. This requires not taking feedback personally, which sometimes feels as if the therapist is unsupportive.

I suggest that support in our work emerges over time in the mutual understanding that I may see things that they may not see or want to see. I may

DOI: 10.4324/9781003649632-5

have a perspective about the way they are going about their lives that may be very hard to hear and digest.

I believe support develops from an environment where there is an openness to say what is difficult to say and an ability to tolerate feedback without taking it personally. I believe that is *support with substance*.

Patients in the Victim Position

Patients in therapy, not infrequently, complain that someone did something untoward to them. Agazarian (personal consultation) called the tendency to blame and complain the *victim position*.

In exploring the experience below the blaming and complaining, we generally find feelings of vulnerability that the patient could not cope with and were consequently split off from awareness. While splitting off awareness of vulnerability, the blaming and complaining frequently provoke aggression, which ironically recreates the vulnerability they are attempting to avoid.

Common examples of the victim position frequently reflect the sentiment that the patient is being treated unfairly. The complaint is expressed in an exaggerated manner, "She always attacks me." "She never listens to me." In looking for the experiences below these statements, more often than not we find some form of vulnerability. "I am sad that I don't know how to get through to her." "I'm afraid I could lose her."

I encourage patients to explore for their experience below their complaints, identify these feelings and experiences, and learn how to express them effectively. I tell patients that the here-and-now experience of the group can give them the opportunity to practice expressing their vulnerability and needs in a way that is more effective than their familiar pattern of blaming and complaining.

Trauma

I was trained to understand that much of our work in therapy deals with the consequences of all forms of trauma. In my practice, I do not specialize in working with particular types of trauma. I find it important to be empathically attuned to the patient no matter what the headline trauma.

I keep in mind:

the *type* of trauma (sexual, physical, emotional),

the *degree* of the trauma (mild, moderate, severe),

the resulting *symptoms* of the trauma (depression, avoidance, fear of dependency/abandonment, etc.) and how to address the underlying causes of these symptoms.

I have worked with patients who reported feeling *objectified* by therapists who would label the patient as a survivor of a particular type of trauma (rape victim, assault victim, abuse victim, etc.).

I believe that we, as therapists, should become familiar with the issues that are common to the patient's particular trauma so as to become more empathically attuned to the patient's experience. I was trained to focus on the underlying experience of the trauma (the helpless, hopeless, rageful, numb experiences) as it relates to the patient's current life.

Often, the group experience, which is focused on the here and now, will generate look-alike events that will activate responses that are experienced as traumatic. These are opportunities that can help patients differentiate between experiences that are the result of look-alike events from actual traumatic experiences in the here and now. Examples are countless, ranging from overwhelmed reactions to a raised voice, to not being able to endure an extended silence in the group.

Some patients are particularly sensitive to interactions with characteristics of specific group members. The group experience gives the patient an opportunity to recognize that many current reactions are the result of look-alike events that mirror their trauma. A goal of the therapy is to help the patient separate out from the grip of their traumatic response to look-alike events, by being "larger than the moment." This work focuses on helping the patient develop the capacity to separate out an observing sense of self from their experiential self.

Some interventions I may utilize focus on the differences in the patient's experience when they were traumatized contrasted with their current experience (Agazarian, 1997).

> "Tell us five ways that Sam is different from your father."

> "What resources do you have now that you didn't have when you were left alone with your uncle?"

Self-Disclosure of the Therapist

During my training, self-disclosure was a topic of considerable controversy. Differing perspectives were considered and supported, ranging from the extreme classical perspective of never revealing anything, to revealing aspects of self in a careful, goal-oriented way (Gorkin, 1987; Wright, 2000). At the other end of the continuum, there were practitioners who believed in revealing a great deal, including what they were experiencing and feeling toward the patients throughout the therapy. They considered self-revealing to be an essential therapeutic tool.

I have found that use of judicious self-disclosure has been extremely helpful in my practice. Self-disclosure for me is a delicate judgment call that takes into account:

the therapeutic alliance I have with the patient,

the goal I have in revealing whatever I might reveal,

the ability of the patient to understand the spirit of why I'm saying what I'm saying.

Early on in my practice, I was much less self-revealing than I have learned to be over time and with experience. Patients would frequently ask me if I was gay or straight, married or single, how old I was, etc. Depending on how insight-oriented I sensed the patient to be, my initial response might be, "What do you need me to be?" I would then explore why they needed me to be gay, straight, married, etc.

Revealing myself immediately would generally result in losing the tension and spontaneity of their response, which could have given us insight into the projections related to their questions. It was a way of introducing them to the nature of their projections.

> Sylvia, whose presenting complaint was that she didn't trust men but wanted to be in a relationship with one, responded that she needed me to be gay. In exploring her need, she revealed that since she had difficulties with men, she thought working with a male therapist would be a more productive match for her. She imagined working with a male therapist would be more emotionally challenging than seeing a female therapist, who, she projected, would be too supportive and less anxiety-provoking for her. Working with a gay male therapist was a tolerable compromise for her at the time, since she was very intimidated by the prospect of working with a straight male therapist.
>
> Interestingly, after a year, Sylvia started a session saying, "I think I need you to be straight now." Again, we explored her need and found that she felt more trusting of me after working together for this period of time. She now wanted to explore her experience thinking of me as a straight male. I never directly revealed if I was straight or gay.

Self-disclosure has been very useful when I have been accused of "making a mistake" or "not being emphatically attuned." I have found that admitting that I had made a mistake or acknowledging that I had not been empathically attuned has been very useful in preserving the therapeutic alliance. I always try to follow up this self-disclosure with an exploration of the patient's experience in witnessing self-disclosure on my part.

An example of self-disclosure that contributed to strengthening the therapeutic alliance was:

> Sue unexpectedly exclaimed, "Arthur, you seem annoyed at me." I was surprised by this remark and responded that I wasn't aware of being annoyed. The moment passed and the group went on to something else.

While the group progressed, I realized that I was, in fact, annoyed with Sue. Shortly afterwards, during a lull in the exchange, I opened up, saying, "I'd like to backtrack for a moment. While I was sitting here quietly, I realized that Sue was correct. I was annoyed with her." Sue, upon hearing me acknowledge her experience, became emotional and choked up.

A group member asked her what was going on and she related through her tears that "It meant a great deal to me that Arthur, who I tend to see as a reliable authority figure, admitted that my perception was valid, even though he couldn't see it at first. In my family, that never happened. If I said something to my parents that made them uncomfortable, they would just dismiss it."

At times, I may use very limited, focused, self-disclosure when a patient opens up to feelings and experiences that no one in the group can or will join.

> An example of this occurred when Mary became furious about a fellow group member "blowing off the group after all the work we did with him." I asked the group if anyone could join Mary's fury. No one responded. After several attempts, I asked Mary what she was experiencing in the group just then. She admitted to feeling "very embarrassed. I should not have said anything. I'm the only one in the group who overreacted that way. What's wrong with me?"

At that point, I decided to join her experience, in kind, not intensity, so that she wasn't left "out on a limb" all by herself. I suggested that I could join her in feeling extremely frustrated when someone I count on seems to be taking me for granted.

This intervention seemed to be a path to opening up a meaningful exploration, as other members began to share their experiences when feeling taken for granted in dependency relationships. My joining Mary in a limited self-disclosure succeeded in her not being isolated at a vulnerable moment, as well as providing energy for other members to explore their reactions and experiences.

When I engage in self-disclosure, I disclose what seems to be appropriate in terms of *process, not content.* When a patient seems extremely shaky or vulnerable, I may, on occasion, share that I have experienced that experience myself in a similar situation.

"Yes, I have felt [jumpy, critical, harsh], when overextended, similar to what you're saying you are experiencing now."

I would *not* say, "Oh, yes, when I was dealing with my mother's illness and trying to deal with my son's difficulties at school, I felt just like you are saying you are feeling now."

I've noticed that self-disclosure does not work very well with patients who have moderate to severe narcissistic features. A response to self-disclosure in this case might be, "I'm not here to talk about you." This response reinforces my understanding that, for this patient, I am basically a utility. I am being related to as a self-object, an extension of the patient. It has been useful to experience and take note of this type of response. It helps me be more emphatically attuned to being able to imagine what it feels like to be the patient in their shoes.

Countertransference

I have found that being familiar with countertransference has helped me approach challenging, confusing, and sometimes therapy-threatening moments in my work. I refer to countertransference in the section describing role locks. It can be helpful to keep this perspective in mind during many challenging moments in our work.

I generally do not have countertransference in the front of my mind until a moment occurs where I experience a heightened awareness of my emotional state that is not in keeping with my normal centered experience facilitating group (Gorkin, 1987). Examples of this include feeling overwhelmed, frightened, angry, very uncomfortable, judgmental, etc. toward a patient or the group as a whole.

A role lock between group members, or between a member and me, is not uncommon. It is helpful for me to refer to these moments as an *enactment*. Enactments, which generally are provoked by role locks, stand out as moments that are experienced with intense emotions that seem disproportionate to what has transpired. When this occurs, I refer to my understanding of how Tansey and Burke (1989) describe Heinrich Racker's approach to countertransference. They focus on two types of identification in countertransference:

Concurrent identification: I am being induced to feel similarly to what the patient is stating they are feeling (e.g., overwhelmed, confused, on fire, scared, low energy, etc.).

Complementary identification: I am being induced to identify and to feel similar to an internalized object representing an important relationship in the patient's life.

The following case illustrates some of these reactions.

Jim came from a high-powered, competitive family. His parents would judge and shame him overtly and covertly if he did not meet their academic and social expectations. He did very well scholastically and excelled in sports. No matter how well he did, however, he would always feel the burden of being constantly evaluated.

Jim achieved a great deal in his life. He had a relatively happy marriage that periodically showed signs of strain, had a son whom he felt close to but was a challenge, and did well professionally as an architect. Despite his external successes, Jim was never satisfied with himself.

Initially we made progress in identifying, recognizing, and working on what we established as the part of him that was driven by perfectionistic strivings. My goal was to introduce and incorporate Winnicott's (1971) focus on being "good enough."

During this period, he reported satisfaction with an improved relationship with his wife and increased self-esteem. He became increasingly able to identify the internal part (voice) that was so harsh, judgmental, and unforgiving. He worked on aiming to be good enough. He reported it was a relief for him not to feel that the world expected him to be perfect.

After two years, he started to feel impatient with his progress. The harsh, judgmental voice was now aimed at me. Our work, although helpful at times, was now not good enough. Over a period of several weeks (which coincided with my preparing to leave on a month's vacation), Jim began to voice how frustrated he was with the pace of his therapy.

Yes, his irritable bowel symptoms were improving but were still there. Yes, his relationship with his wife was improving, but he still would get impatient with her and start a quarrel related to his being dissatisfied with her behavior. Yes, his continuous worry had dissipated but still had a grip on him. Still, his progress in therapy was not good enough.

During this period, I would respond to his complaints with my usual suggestion that we explore his experience. I would bring up the work we had done with the part of him that could be harsh and judgmental. I asked him what his experience was like in not moving fast enough in his therapy. He sharply responded, "I'm not interested in 'exploring' anything. I'm not interested in exploring 'my experience.' Stop giving me this 'therapy talk'."

In attempting to engage his observing ego and find our therapeutic alliance, I suggested that perhaps his harsh critical voice is coming out now for some reason and being aimed at me. Again, he dismissed this as just me defending myself.

His relentless attacks were having an effect on me. I reflected on my heightened affect and considered this to be an experience of induced concurrent countertransference. He was not progressing fast enough, and I was not a good-enough therapist.

He increased his attacks. He would add up how much his therapy cost over the previous two years and let me know he expected that he would be further along in his therapy. "After spending all these thousands of dollars, I'm still doing the same things." No matter what intervention I used, his harsh judgment and attacks would not budge. I couldn't elicit his observing ego.

During this three-week episode, I experienced myself moving from induced feelings of defensiveness to frustration to impotence related to a sense that maybe he wasn't progressing as much as I thought. I started to experience myself making an internal shift from judging myself as not being good enough (concurrent countertransference) to judging him. Taking a step back, I began to view my reaction as an example of complementary countertransference. I imagined that I was feeling similar to the person in his life, an internalized object, who would judge him.

After being dismissed countless times, I finally suggested that maybe he had a point, maybe we had reached a dead end in our work. Perhaps another kind of therapy would be more productive.

His response, in an even-tempered voice that was filled with contempt, was, "Are you kidding? After spending $10,000 on my therapy with you, I'm not going anywhere." At this point, after three weeks of relentless attacks, I realized that I felt entirely powerless. I couldn't find a way to get through to Jim. I couldn't even get rid of him. I felt *completely impotent*.

At that moment, I took a step back from my personal experience and hypothesized that I was being induced into feeling impotent (concordant countertransference). I imagined that I was feeling very similar to what my patient was feeling. I utilized this insight (not very hopeful that it would work, since nothing else did) and said, "I think I finally understand emotionally the depth of what you're communicating to me. I'm at this moment feeling completely impotent."

He stared at me quietly for an extended moment. I had no idea what to expect. Suddenly he then gave me a big smile and said, "Wow, I think I needed you to feel that. Thank you for being so honest with me. Finally, I feel understood."

This successful therapeutic episode, utilizing what I understood to be my induced countertransference reactions as a tool, opened up his therapy.

Jim has been with me for many years, doing very well. He periodically refers back to this episode as having been very significant for him in feeling relieved that he did not kill me off (as had happened in other dependency relationships), and I did not kill him off (as had happened in other important dependency relationships).

Approaching Dreams in Group

I was trained to consider dreams as having actually happened. They happened either metaphorically or realistically. I propose to the group that we approach dreams with this in mind. I suggest that the patient wrote the script of the dream. I ask why they imagine they wrote this script now. I advise that the dream should reflect the themes we are working on in therapy.

Once a group member shares the dream with the group, it becomes a group dream. I recommend that instead of analyzing the dream we should try to relate to it through our own experiences.

"What's your experience like as you listen to Mary share her dream?"

"What meaning would the dream have for you right now, if *you* dreamt it?"

"If this is your dream, what is it telling you about you?"

I attempt to interweave the theme of the dream with the patient's presenting complaints and group goals (Yalom & Leszcz, 2005). I explore to see if the dreamer is dreaming this dream for the group. I ask the group how (not if) the dream reflects their group experience.

> Pat brings in a dream. "I came to group. Your office was three times as large as it normally is. There were twenty people in the office sitting in the circle. We were all waiting for you silently."
>
> In exploring the dream, several members related feeling the anxiety of getting lost in the group. Some feared I would add more members to the group. Several wanted more members in the group.
>
> Pat, the group member who brought in the dream, related it to her early family experiences of being the third of four siblings. A theme in her therapy was related to her feeling "I don't matter."
>
> The dream seemed to help Pat understand why she often felt so uncomfortable in group. She acknowledged to the group that her group-mates were becoming more important to her. The more important the group became, the more her fear that she didn't matter became apparent.
>
> She experienced great reluctance to admit this to the group. She also came to the realization that she had trouble admitting it to herself. She defended herself with a posture of pseudo-self-sufficiency, having a tendency to convince herself that she didn't matter to others and others did not really matter to her.

Understanding the dream in this way facilitated a great deal of exploration regarding what the group meant to other members, as well as what members meant to each other.

Chapter 6

Frames of Reference

I have found that using certain frames of reference helps patients comprehend the perspective I have adopted in my practice of therapy. Some frames are more concrete, some more abstract; frequently, they are existential.

All Behavior Has a Purpose

Group therapy, being the fishbowl that it is, frequently leads patients to feeling self-conscious, embarrassed, empowered, shamed, relieved, etc. In preparing patients to make the best use of their group experience, I counsel patients to approach our work by adopting two perspectives. One is the perspective and experience of the *observing self* (Greenson, 1967). The other is the actual experience or, as we say, the *experiential self*. In doing this, we want to take a step back, observe, understand, and learn from the experience of our participation in group.

At this point, I introduce the notion that *all behavior has a purpose*. I find that highlighting this notion helps patients become more interested in taking on the observer role and not taking what they are experiencing in group personally.

Periodically, I will point out that all behavior has a purpose. "What do you imagine is the purpose of your (fighting, avoidance, sarcasm, lateness, silence, etc.)?" This question is especially useful when pointing out and exploring behaviors that are self-defeating. It can help the patient take in feedback that may be difficult to hear (Ormont, 1992).

Me/Not Me

I have found the expression "me/not me" to be a succinct and effective way of indicating that the patient is challenged in not being able to remain separate in a dependency relationship (Winnicott, 1971). I have utilized this expression to reinforce the awareness that "the person that you are relating to is not you. That person may not see things the way you do, may not experience things the way you do, may not feel the way you do."

DOI: 10.4324/9781003649632-6

This may seem obvious at first. Over time, patients recognize how often they are projecting into or merging with the individual they are relating to. I have had many patients report that this phrase has become a useful shortcut in helping them recognize when they are not being empathically attuned and staying separate from the person they are relating to.

Empathic Attunement

Empathy, in the way I work, requires that we resonate with how we imagine the person we are relating to, knowing what we know of this person, is feeling and experiencing in this moment (Yalom & Leszcz, 2005). Empathy, as I understand it, is the attempt to imagine how *they* feel "in their shoes," not imagining how *we* would feel in their shoes, which I recognize as *identification*.

This simple change in perspective is not so obvious to many patients or therapists. They seem to conflate empathy with being kind, caring, and sympathetic. Patients, when conceptualizing empathy in this way, frequently report that they find themselves being more successful in relating and communicating effectively.

Know Your Chickens

In clarifying how I understand empathic attunement, I will frequently introduce the sentiment behind the Italian idiom "know your chickens." This generally means, in a lighthearted way, that in order to be empathically attuned I have to imagine how the other person is feeling in their shoes, not how I would feel.

"Knowing your chickens" signifies that we should take into account the specific, known idiosyncrasies of the person we are relating to, just as the farmer knows the particular attributes and habits of his particular chickens, when attempting to be empathically attuned.

Disbelieving the Patient

A patient will often ask me if I believe them. I first ask what prompted the question. They generally say something to the effect that they saw some expression on my face. I ask, "What did you see in my face?" The answer usually is some form of, "I thought you didn't believe me."

An exploration usually reveals some sort of projection related to issues of trust. I say to them that in my training I was taught not to believe or disbelieve what is being said. My focus is on what is the meaning of their communication, and not on whether I believe them (Greenson, 1967). Many patients report that they feel freed up by this notion because they don't have to worry if they are communicating their experience accurately. Some patients get confused by this posture, and so I explore this further with them.

Riley, a 45-year-old advertising executive, entered therapy to deal with depression. She had been in treatment with several therapists, who were supportive but not helpful with her recurring low mood and feelings of hopelessness. She was on a high dosage of Zoloft, which seemed to help somewhat, but she still found herself periodically thinking of suicide (which she insisted were only thoughts).

As we explored her previous therapy, she recounted how her last therapist helped her make sense of some of her despair. Her therapist was trained in exploring for "recovered memories." During her explorations, she "remembered" having been molested in her teenage years by a number of family members, including her father, grandmother, and uncles. She also recounted her family being part of a cult that would assemble in her house and have rituals she described as terrifying. When I would ask for details about these memories, much of what she recounted didn't add up.

At some point, Riley looked at me and inquired, "Do you believe me?" I responded that I was trained not to believe or disbelieve what my patients tell me. I told her that my way of working had to do with the meaning of what she was bringing into her therapy. I told her that my focus is always on what a patient's goal is in their therapy. Was her goal to be believed? Was her goal to deal with her depression, which I suggested had to do with hopelessness, helplessness, and low self-esteem related to a lack of mastery in attachments? What did it mean to her to be believed? What did it mean to her not to be believed?

I asked Riley why she left her previous therapist. She replied that even though he helped her "remember" what she erased from awareness, her depression and general sense of despair never changed. She had continued in therapy with me for six months when I suggested that she join one of my groups. She was very apprehensive. She was worried that no one would believe her. I suggested again that in our work the issue is not to believe or disbelieve each other. Our work in group is to observe and learn how we contribute to the problems we are in therapy to work on.

Riley joined the group. She brought in her recovered memories. The group explored their reactions to what they were hearing. I reminded the group that we were here to focus on the here and now. Our perspective is not to believe or disbelieve each other. Our focus is always on our goals in therapy and how we are contributing to the problems we are working on. After an initial period, when the group focused on the content of Riley's recovered memories and their reactions, the issue receded into the background.

Riley stayed in the group for several years. As we explored her "nickel in the dime" related to her depression, we noticed that she had a tendency in group to use language in a way that seemed to exaggerate what she felt and experienced. She often would say she "felt suicidal" when she felt uncomfortable with feedback directed to her. I would ask if these were suicidal thoughts or actual plans to go through with killing herself. She would respond that they were thoughts and wanted to reassure everyone that she did not intend to actually kill herself. It was just how she felt.

The group explored the impact of her saying that she was "feeling suicidal." Several of her groupmates shared that they were concerned about giving Riley feedback that might upset her out of concern that she would kill herself as a result. Several members said that they felt cautious with Riley and tended to tiptoe around her. Hearing this feedback upset Riley, but also seemed to surprise her.

In exploring her experience, she revealed that her husband would say the same thing. When upset with him, she would tend to cry and tell him she wanted to kill herself. As time passed, he seemed not to take her seriously anymore. However, she did feel that he tiptoed around her much of the time, leading to arguments where she would accuse him of "holding back" and not telling her "the truth." There did seem to be an obvious parallel process. When upset in group, and with her husband, she would express her upset in ways that stopped all communication.

I suggested that, since she was clear that she didn't want to kill herself, would she agree not to say the word *suicide* unless she really meant to go through with it? I proposed that when she thought about wanting to kill herself she try to explore for the feeling below the words and sentiment.

She agreed not to use the word *suicide*. She would try to find language that might be more effective in not scaring others. I took that to mean that she was giving therapy a chance to deal with her inability to communicate her distress to others without alienating and overwhelming them.

Soon afterward, we established a mutual assumption. She recognized that she would become very desperate and "suicidal" as a result of not believing she could get the attention of those she needed in her life to understand and appreciate what she was going through. She would try to communicate her distress, but would do it in a way that overwhelmed those on whom she depended.

In our exploration of what we established as her dysfunctional "pay attention to me" role, we found that this role was developed as a child in her family of origin. Riley was the third of four siblings, who were always competing for the attention of their overwhelmed mother. She found a reliable solution to getting attention was with exaggerated calls for help.

One example was to say she was feeling ill when she was upset about something. She noticed that her mother would respond to the children when they were physically sick. When nothing was found to be wrong, her mother would berate her for "making it up." Being negatively responded to was better than not being noticed at all. Ultimately, she felt isolated, alone, and worthless.

Riley was encouraged to notice her experience when she felt overlooked, wanted attention, or was feeling upset about something in the group. Her work was to explore below her initial responses, which would frequently be provocative. She gradually recognized that her unexpressed need for attention and her desire to belong would be obscured by her saying something that would distract, annoy, or provoke other group members.

She held onto her agreement not to use the word *suicide* unless she was serious about it. Over time she reported feeling less depressed and despairing, even though her depression never left her entirely. She recognized how she contributed to problems with her husband by being difficult, disagreeable, and provocative.

She practiced showing her vulnerability by stating her desires and needs to him instead of complaining, putting him down, having a fight, and ultimately working herself up to the point of telling him that she wanted to kill herself. She reported that the "ice was melting" between them.

Riley left the group after four years. During the termination, she expressed gratitude for the work she accomplished. She brought up how she appreciated that she felt less depressed, even though we did not focus on her trauma related to her "recovered memories." She still wondered if I and the group believed her.

There Is No Objective Reality

As I mentioned above, in the process of exploring experience in group and outside of group, I take on the posture of neither believing nor disbelieving what someone says. Of course, we take seriously what a group member may say or report. However, that is only the beginning of the process of understanding each other in group.

I often suggest that in our work there is no objective reality. The responses I receive to this proposition range from patients arguing that of course there is an objective reality, to those who become interested in exploring what I mean.

PATIENT: "What does it mean there is no objective reality in our work?"
ARTHUR: [pointing to the ottoman] "What is this?"
PATIENT: "It's an ottoman."
ARTHUR: "OK. However, if I threw it out the window from my 16th-floor office and it landed on someone's head, what would it be?"
PATIENT: "It's still an ottoman."
ARTHUR: "No, it would be a missile."

I try to clarify the difference between *connotation* and *denotation*. The words ottoman, fear, love, depression, etc. all express the literal meaning, the *denotation* of what we are trying to communicate. *Connotation* refers to the ideas, feelings, experiences, and emotions we think of when we hear a particular word. The challenge is to comprehend and clarify what denotations connote.

I suggest that anger, depression, and happiness mean many different things to different people. In group, we try to find the connotation of what we or others are expressing by exploring what is below and within the feelings or experiences we are reporting.

Look-Alike Events

I have always looked for simple phrases to help patients recognize common processes that occur in our therapeutic explorations. These tend to aid in developing mutual assumptions and become shortcuts in our therapeutic language. One very helpful frame that I borrowed from Agazarian (personal consultation) is the recognition of a *look-alike event*.

The look-alike event is generally an occurrence or event that triggers an exaggerated response in the patient related to trauma that the patient has experienced in their past. When this happens, I find it helpful to point out to patients that they seem to be experiencing an intense reaction to something that occurred in the group because of a look-alike event. This approach generally helps the patient take in feedback by reducing the shame related to an event that induced an exaggerated reaction in them.

Making the Relationship More Important than the Content

Frequently, group members will find themselves in a role lock that reflects the same undermining pattern they at times experience in their outside lives. One pattern that I've seen contributing to this outcome occurs when a group member is more focused on getting their point across than recognizing the effect they are having on the person they are relating (or not relating) to.

In exploring their experience, group members frequently insist that they feel misunderstood, wiped out, dismissed (all *victim* complaints). They insist on pushing their content rather than noticing the process between themselves and the person they are trying to affect. The intervention of, "It seems that you're more concerned about getting your point across than how you're affecting the person you want to be understood by. Is this working for you?" frequently arouses the patient's curiosity.

JACK: "Shouldn't I be understood?"

ARTHUR: "That's a legitimate goal. However, the way you're going about it seems to lead you to fight."

JACK: "OK, so what do I do now?"

ARTHUR: "Maybe consider the way you're affecting Jill being as important or even more important than the content. Jill, what do you think?"

JILL: "It would be easier to swallow what he's saying if he didn't have such a dismissive tone and try to force feed me."

ARTHUR: "Jack, did you realize that the way you were speaking to Jill actually interfered with your getting your point across?"

JACK: "No."

Should We Care about Our Patients?

At some point during my own experience in therapy, I complained to my therapist that he didn't seem to care about me. I'll never forget his response, which was, "Am I supposed to?" His response helped me to realize that I was looking for affection, admiration, and love from him. We explored my needs, and how I could project these needs into inappropriate relationships (usually male authority figures) that would ultimately disappoint me.

Working with supervisees and consultees over the years, many have reported finding themselves in a bind with their patients because of their taking on a caring role. Some consultees report that they cared about their patients without exploring what it meant to them. They believe that they *should* care, they were *supposed to* care about their patients. Gradually over time, they would begin to feel very burdened by it.

> In one example, my supervisee, Ed, recognized that he would lose track of his goals and the patient's goals in the therapy. Instead of exploring and helping his patients discover what was holding them back from reaching their goals, he relied on giving advice and providing support. At first, this would be very rewarding for both Ed and his patient. The patient would report feeling more hopeful and enthusiastic. Ed would feel satisfied that the therapy was "progressing."
>
> Over time, the therapy would meander, focusing on the headline issue of the week. Ed found himself reluctant to give his patients challenging feedback out of fear that they would become upset. The therapy would become stagnant. Ed would report feeling trapped by the concern that the patient would feel unsupported, uncared for, and, even worse, blamed by feedback that could be perceived as critical. He had never established a therapeutic alliance where he could give his patients feedback without their taking the feedback personally.

When interviewing new referrals who were previously in treatment. I generally ask, "What didn't work in your last therapy?" Ironically, upon exploring why new referrals left their former therapists, I would frequently hear about situations similar to Ed's from the perspective of the patient. They would complain that their therapy "hit a dead end" with the former therapist.

In exploring this question, patients would begin to realize that they tended to hold back negative reactions toward their former therapist. They would be concerned that their therapist's feelings would be hurt. They would report fearing that they would jeopardize the relationship with the one person who "cared" for them.

Patients would frequently report that it was difficult to end therapy with their former therapist because they cared for the therapist and felt cared for. They didn't want to hurt the therapist's feelings. I use this as an opportunity to suggest that I want to prevent this pattern from developing into a barrier between us. I propose establishing an agreement between us where I can give them feedback and also count on them to give me feedback without taking this feedback personally.

If and when the question comes up about my caring for a patient, I open it up for exploration. What does it mean for the patient that it appears I care or don't care for them? What would it feel like if they knew I cared for them? What could be the downside in my caring for them? If the patient persists in wanting to know if I cared about them, I say that my caring is focused on the mutual success of our work,

Support Groups

In my practice, I do not lead support groups or homogeneous groups. Support groups have become increasingly popular over the past forty years. When I started my practice in the early 1980s, these groups (divorced men, divorced women, gay, lesbian, new fathers, new mothers, bereavement, trauma, etc.) were popular with group therapists as a way to carve out a niche for their practice.

These groups seem to be attractive to people because they appear to offer a sense of safety. Many people have reported benefiting from participating in a safe environment where they encountered and shared similar life experiences.

Over the years, I have had quite a few patients referred to me after having had surprisingly difficult, sometimes quite negative experiences in these types of support groups. In my experience, after an initial experience of enchantment when members feel a sense of closeness, mutual understanding, and safety (based on the illusion of "sameness"), underlying dynamics common to all groups emerge based on not being able to tolerate differences.

Over time, it is common for group members to find themselves holding back from sharing differences. These differences (different opinions, sentiments, perspectives, reactions) are frequently overtly or more often subtly "bullied" away. Patients learn not to speak up out of fear of being shamed or even scapegoated. This experience often leads to a tendency to "join" stereotypical subgroups that develop into a pseudo-bonding among group members.

I have had more than a few patients say they were reluctant to join group therapy. Upon exploration, I frequently found that they had attended some sort of support or homogeneous group where they were afraid to open up when they felt differently than their groupmates. They would report feeling inhibited in sharing their experience if it didn't echo what others were sharing.

They were concerned that my way of facilitating the group would expose them to a similar, unrewarding experience.

I respond that after going through an experience that they described as unhelpful I can understand their reluctance to join one of my groups. I ask them to give it a chance. I clarify that one of the goals in group therapy is to "say everything," whether or not they believe it will be supported. "If you can't say everything, at least let us know there is something you are not saying so that we can explore why you are not revealing it. Why you can't or won't reveal it is more important than the content of what you can't reveal."

This approach has been generally successful in allaying the initial fears of patients who had participated in groups where they expected safety and found themselves unexpectedly feeling unsafe.

What Didn't Work in Your Last Therapy?

This question has been very useful in discovering what specific challenges I should be on the lookout for when working with a new patient (Rutan & Stone, 2001). I always ask this question at the end of an initial consultation if we decide to work together. Patients' responses have been very helpful in discovering how the previous therapist related to the patient in ways that did not work. It helps me build on those therapeutic failures, so I don't repeat them.

Common responses to this inquiry are:

1. "My therapist was so very nice and supportive, but we weren't getting anywhere. I didn't have the heart to tell him when I disagreed, didn't understand, or didn't trust what he was saying."

This response was not uncommon among patients who consulted with me before telling their former therapist that they wanted to end therapy and consult with someone else. I would tell this potential patient that I wouldn't consider beginning therapy with them until they told their therapist that they wanted to leave and went through a termination. Not infrequently they would tell their therapist. The termination would inevitably be brief and abortive.

2. "He helped me understand why I am the way I am, but nothing changed."

This response usually leads me to suggest group therapy as an adjunct to their individual work and why it can help when individual therapy reaches a dead end.

3. "She was always a few minutes late to session. It left me with the sense that I wasn't that important to her. It also seemed that her boundaries weren't reliable. How was she going to help me with mine?"

Inevitably, the exploration would expand into whether or not the patient communicated their reactions to the therapist. Frequently, they had not shared their thoughts and feelings with their therapist. This provided me with the opportunity to explore why they didn't. It led me to introduce the norm of saying everything and "If you can't, at least let me know that there's something you're experiencing or thinking but are reluctant to say. It's more important to explore why you won't share what you are experiencing than the content of what you won't or can't reveal."

4. "He kept asking me how I feel about this, how I feel about that. I didn't understand how that was going to help me. He kept saying it was important to know how I felt. He never told me, and I never asked him why it was important. I didn't see the point. I hope you're not going to ask me over and over again, 'So what do you feel?'"

This response generally leads me to some psychoeducation about the value of knowing what you feel. I give examples of work I've done with patients to clarify how the ability to recognize and identify feelings and resulting experiences is vital to the therapeutic process.

Cate, a 55-year-old, married, high-level administrator in city government, had been in individual treatment with two therapists focusing on her presenting complaint regarding the polarized relationship she had with her husband.

I asked Cate about her previous therapy. She complained that both therapists "were useless." Both kept asking her how she "felt about this, felt about that." She didn't see the point. The therapy was "too touchy-feely" and seemed unfocused. She spent several months with each, but left both therapists, complaining "I'm not getting anywhere."

Hearing Cate's complaints about her previous therapy prepared me for the possibility of falling into the same trap. I made it a point to clarify, very early on in her therapy, when and why I ask for feelings and how it helps us in our work. "Being aware of our experience, which emerges from our feeling state, can provide us with a better sense of why you do what you do that might be interfering with your getting to your goal of seeing how you contribute to the problems you're having with your husband."

Cate, who valued being very practical, no-nonsense and goal-oriented, seemed open to what she called "your approach to feelings." She smiled at me, saying "I don't go for this touchy-feely stuff." I suggested that she enter one of my groups as an adjunct to her individual sessions. She agreed to it. She was curious about group since she heard it was helpful to a friend of hers.

In group, we began to recognize a pattern revealing a tendency to elevate herself and at times talk down to the person she was relating to. This occurred regularly with Joan, who had a tendency to be tangential in her responses and ramble. Cate would also communicate her impatience non-verbally by raising her eyebrows. When I asked her if she noticed that she was making a face, she replied that she did not realize that it was so obvious.

I asked the group if they noticed Cate's expression while Joan was talking. Several suggested that Cate's gestures were obvious and very provocative. Joan shared that she was furious with Cate. I suggested that this was an opportunity for her to explore the feelings that were communicated in her nonverbal making-a-face gesture.

ARTHUR: "Can you take a moment and see what feelings are being com-municated in your raised eyebrows?"

CATE: "Isn't it obvious?"

ARTHUR: "Can you put words to it?"

CATE: "I'm embarrassed to say it out loud."

ARTHUR: "It seems that it's being noticed whether or not you say it openly. Remember that an important part of our work is to commu-nicate effectively. Are you being effective in communicating your feelings by making a face?"

CATE: "Apparently not."

Cate sheepishly went on to admit that she was feeling impatient and judgmental toward Joan. I asked what she was feeling below the judg-ment. She again hesitated and said she had a thought, not a feeling. I asked her to reveal her thoughts. She looked at Joan and said, "I hope you don't take this personally. I feel this with a lot of people I count on. The thought is, 'You're useless'."

Remembering that she described her former therapists as useless, I suggested that it seemed she had a harsh, punitive part of her that came out at times. I asked her if she could take a moment and reflect on her experience of someone being useless.

After a long moment, she smiled sadly and admitted that this was how she felt toward her self-centered and distracted mother. She went on to describe an example of how she could not count on her mother to take her anywhere on time. "I was always the last kid waiting for my mom to pick me up from school at the end of the day. I always felt scared that she would forget me. She would always finally come, apologizing. I always felt I had to say it was okay, but it wasn't okay." Group members, including Joan, showed acceptance and support as she revealed a childhood where she became pseudo-self-sufficient and resented it.

Cate began to realize that the way she talked down to her groupmates paralleled the frequent interactions she had with her husband. Her voice would inevitably take on an elevated, impatient tone. The content of their arguments frequently focused on differences of opinion as to how to raise their two young boys. She became aware of a feeling of "depending on someone I can't rely on."

Cate was beginning to understand her contribution to her complaints, her "nickel in the dime." She became aware of a tightness in her throat that was a signal of discomfort with what she was hearing. She developed a curiosity about what was being said, instead of cutting the person off mid-sentence and arguing a point that may not have even been articulated. She became more aware of her tone of voice, which could be nasty when she felt frustrated. Cate learned to express, in a variety of ways, not feeling comfortable with what the other person said rather than expressing disdain at what was being said.

Over time, Cate reported using what she learned in group. She acknowledged that her group work was changing the way she felt toward her husband. She couldn't understand why they were growing apart. Now at least Cate knew how she was contributing to the problem.

In general, exploring what went wrong in a patient's previous therapy has helped me in identifying what to look out for in my beginning work with a new patient. It provides me with a bit of a roadmap for how to avoid the same rabbit holes that the former therapist fell into. It has been an extremely useful therapeutic tool.

Chapter 7

Therapeutic Stance with Patients

Your Nickel in the Dime

Patients in group frequently start off complaining about or blaming someone else for problems they are facing in their lives. One frame that I borrowed from Brian, a consultee of mine, is to ask patients in the group, "So what's your nickel in the dime?"

At first, this perspective confuses most patients. However, after suggesting that our therapy is focused on how we are contributing to the problems we are complaining about, asking "What is your nickel in the dime?" can give patients a sense of hope in their therapy. I try to help them understand that it is quite difficult, if not impossible, to change another person. Our goal in therapy is to understand how we are contributing to the problem. This change in perspective gives us the opportunity to recognize how we may be more productive in affecting the situations we are complaining about.

"How are you contributing to the problems you are bringing to your therapy?" This question, which seems to free up many patients, can also make some patients feel very uncomfortable. It is not uncommon for a new group member to misunderstand this posture as a form of "blaming the victim." I am very careful to explore the patient's reaction to hearing this and make sure that they understand the sentiment behind it.

Bad things do happen to us. However, our goal in therapy is to recognize, understand, and deal with the effects of dysfunctional roles and trauma, which frequently take the form of the issues patients present with.

I then introduce the idea that *all behavior has a purpose*. Of course, we are not going to examine all their behaviors. However, I find it helps reduce the patient's shame and embarrassment when they realize that their self-defeating behaviors are purposeful and at one time may have even been functional (Ormont, 1992).

In establishing the notion that all behavior has a purpose, I suggest that we can begin to understand what is interfering with the patient reaching their goals. Keeping the patient's goals at the forefront of our work also tends to give me leverage when the patient's defenses inevitably emerge.

DOI: 10.4324/9781003649632-7

"What is your goal? If you proceed this way, will it get you closer to or further away from your goal?"

Observing Self/Experiential Self

I introduce a therapeutic perspective in which the patient is encouraged to develop an *observing self*, as contrasted to the *experiential self* (Greenson, 1967). The ability to develop an observing-self perspective requires the patient to learn not to take feedback personally (Agazarian, 1997).

I suggest that feedback frequently stings. Our goal is to tolerate the discomfort in hearing difficult feedback. We are attempting to take an emotional step back and to be open to what is being said to us about our behavior and/ or the effect we are having on others. The development of the capacity to take in feedback is a fundamental condition in enabling patients to observe themselves. Being able to observe themselves is the initial challenge in recognizing how they affect others in the world.

Differentiating the Therapeutic Alliance from a Positive Transference

The relationship between the patient's observing self and the therapist's therapeutic-self perspective is the basis of what we understand to be the *therapeutic alliance* (Greenson, 1967). This alliance is what we need when a positive transference turns negative or develops into a fixed transference that never changes.

The therapeutic alliance is not the same as a *positive transference*. A positive transference, which can be very pleasant for both patient and therapist (as experienced therapists know), can flip into a negative transference, abortively, at any time. When it does, we have no leverage, no alliance, no perspective that is larger than the moment being experienced by the therapist and patient.

As I see it, our work, to a large extent, is to provide the patient with a perspective that is different from theirs. That is why they are coming into therapy in the first place. It is our challenge as well as our leverage. The therapeutic alliance facilitates our ability to engage the patient's defenses when they inevitably emerge.

In order to build a therapeutic alliance, it is essential for the therapist to help the patient develop an ability not to take feedback personally. This generally takes a good bit of time and reinforcement. I continually reaffirm this posture throughout the group experience by reminding patients that part of our work is to build tolerance for challenging feedback and not take this feedback personally. This process is easy for most patients to understand intellectually, but not so easy to experience emotionally.

I suggest that we are both the scientist and the guinea pig in our group work. The scientist (observing self) part of us is noticing what we do and feel (the experiential self) as we participate in the group experience (Agazarian, 1997). This process facilitates the ability to learn "What is my nickel in the dime? How am I contributing to the things I'm complaining about?"

One way to help patients not take feedback personally is to help them become familiar with *group-as-a-whole* concepts. I suggest to patients that one member can be the "container" for another member's feelings, or even contain an experience for the whole group.

> "It seems you are containing the group's desire for closeness."

> "It seems that Bill is containing the group's aggression tonight."

I try to help patients understand that, frequently, strong feelings can represent a patient's being the container of that experience for the whole group, in the same way that they were the container for these feelings in the family.

Establishing Mutual Assumptions

As an outgrowth of the therapeutic alliance, I make it a priority to establish mutual assumptions and themes with patients. An example could be the mutual assumption that the patient becomes angry, aggressive, avoidant, confusing, chaotic, passive aggressive, etc. when they feel hurt, uncertain, overwhelmed, judged, etc.

The assumption is generally useless if it isn't mutually agreed upon. Once it is, it can be used as a building block and leverage in the patient's therapeutic toolbox.

General Therapeutic Posture and Interventions

In my work, I rarely interpret. Instead, I present hunches as to what I think I see. I then use that hunch as being the basis of a mutual assumption that then can be used in understanding how the patient, under stress, defensively relates to the world. These are some questions I might ask:

> "Can we pause for a moment and remember what brought you to therapy? I have a hunch that it is related to what is happening in the group right now."

> "Are you getting closer to or further away from your goal?"

> "Can I Interrupt you for a moment and slow us down? Do you remember why I recommended that you start group in the first place? You said that you wanted to work on [speaking up for yourself, managing conflict, controlling your anger, etc.]."

"If you continue this way, will it get you closer to or further away from your goal?"

"An important undertaking in our work is to artificially split our experience into two. One part of us is going to experience what we are experiencing. Another part is going to observe our experience from a bit of distance. Does that make sense?"

"What would happen here if you considered John's point of view?"

"What part of you are you protecting by dismissing Mary's feedback?"

ARTHUR: "What's below your anger, your judgment, your hesitation, etc.?"
PATIENT: "I don't know."
ARTHUR: "If you did know, what would it be?"
ARTHUR: "What are you trying to achieve by engaging in this way?"
TIM: "I want to be understood."
ARTHUR: "Is it OK for me to check something out with the group?"
TIM: "Sure."
ARTHUR: "Is Tim reaching his goal of having you understand him better?"

Reinforcement of Perspectives, Patterns, and Mutual Assumptions

As I reflected on how to present the material in this book, I realized that much of the basic material I'm covering comes up repeatedly in treatment, generally needs reinforcement, and can sometimes seem redundant. What I've experienced is that patients frequently understand what we are saying to them intellectually. It's another thing to have them integrate what they think they understand experientially.

This process initially requires that I repeat and reinforce therapeutic themes until patients can utilize this new perspective on their own. I attempt to take on the role of becoming the container of discovery, insight, and learning until the patient can remember and use them on their own (Agazarian, 1997).

I noticed that, at times, I repeat themes in the body of the book that have already been addressed but generally will come up again at different times in the treatment. If it seems repetitive, I suggest just skipping that section. Compiling and clarifying the issues in this book for me is similar to conducting therapy. It doesn't unfold in a straight line. However, in my experience, it does require gentle and clear reinforcement of basic themes at appropriate moments.

Initial Consultation

During an initial consultation, my primary concern is to understand why this person is seeking therapy. What is their presenting complaint? Early on in our engagement I attempt to translate their presenting complaints into therapeutic goals (Rutan & Stone, 2001).

During our first contact, I generally, in a friendly tone, point out that this is a consultation where we are interviewing each other. Patients are sometimes surprised to hear that I am interviewing them while they are interviewing me. This seems to surprise potential patients who think that the therapy begins as soon as they walk in the door. I tell them I am attempting to get a sense of whether there is a good fit between us.

During the consultation, I want to ascertain if the patient has the capacity to look at him- or herself. Can the patient take in feedback? Are they only looking for support or a short-term solution? Are they looking for enduring change? (Yalom & Leszcz, 2005).

If we decide to work together, I keep the presenting complaint/goal actively in mind. It helps me to stay focused on the patient's purpose in seeking therapy, which can sometimes fade into the background. It provides a clear reference point to hold onto when the therapy seems meandering, stuck, or polarized.

Therapeutic goals change over time, but holding onto the evolving presenting complaints and therapeutic goals gives me a continued frame of reference when defenses inevitably show up. Over time, I've noticed that many consultees I've worked with have no clear idea what they are working on with their patient. They have gotten lost in the content or "headlines of the week" and lose focus on why the patient is there. They realize that the therapy has become generally supportive without having clarity on what they are working on.

General Interview Questions

Current life situation: Family and work relationships.
 Family of origin:

> "Tell me about your family growing up. What was your role in the family? Peacemaker, rebel, quiet one, savior, last hope, etc.?"

> "What roles do you tend to take with people you are intimate with? When you are in new situations?"

> "How did your family deal with conflict [addressing problems directly, avoidance, fighting, blaming, complaining]?"

> "How do you typically deal with criticism?"

> "How were your needs met in your family?"

Previous group experiences:

> "What has been your previous experience in groups? In college, at work? What roles have you taken on and how did they impact you?"

Negative group experiences:

"Have you had any negative experiences in groups, not only therapy groups. It could be school, sports, or friends groups. What happened? Were you scapegoated, cast out, picked on, seen as bad, etc.?"

Medications:

It is essential to know what, if any, medications the patient is taking. Dosage? Who is prescribing the medication?

Previous and current therapy experience:

"Have you been in therapy in the past and for how long? If so, how did it end?" (This can be a good indicator of what may lie down the road.)

Is the patient in therapy with another therapist (Concurrent Psychotherapy)? Consult with the individual therapist.

Was it the therapist's idea, or did the patient seek out group on their own? I clarify how I work and what my goals are for our mutual patient. Does it correspond to the patient's individual treatment? I find it to be important to set a tone of collaborative treatment together, as splitting frequently occurs.

Chapter 8

Practical Considerations

To Zoom or Not to Zoom: Dealing with Technology

On March 13, 2020, COVID-19 was declared a national emergency in the US. Before that date I never paid much attention to telehealth or had the need to engage in it. Since that day, I have worked exclusively using the internet to provide the forum to facilitate my groups. The platform that I found most accessible and convenient was offered by Zoom.

At first, I was very uncertain as to the effectiveness of facilitating group therapy through a telehealth platform. Setting up my group practice on Zoom was surprisingly uneventful and efficient. I was able to conduct my groups missing only one week of sessions. Group members were able to have access to their group experience without risking catching COVID, which at that time was an extremely threatening unknown.

I didn't know what to expect as to how group members were going to respond to this significant change in the format of the group. No waiting room, no office creating a sense of privacy and confidentiality, and dialing in from home were now the new norms. I had no idea how long this transition to telehealth would last, but I was determined to use my experience to deal with whatever came up in the group process.

Group members brought in their reactions to the threats they were facing, as well as adjusting to this new way of working in group. Group members presented with their typical characterological patterns. Those who joked under stress could be counted on to come up with a quip. Those who went silent under stress would tend to go silent. Those who would go into fight roles (generally with the authority, me) tended to go into a fight role. Those who complained about my elevators at the office were often the same patients who complained about meeting on Zoom.

FRANK: "I don't think I like this way of working. I feel like I'm on *Hollywood Squares*" [a television show eerily similar to what members would see on their computer screens when looking at their groupmates]. "This is not going to work!"

DOI: 10.4324/9781003649632-8

ARTHUR: "OK, Frank, could you take a moment and go below your thoughts and see what you're experiencing in your heart?"

FRANK: "Nothing. Nothing is in my heart."

ARTHUR: "Try to take another moment."

[Silence in the group]

FRANK: "I'm really scared. I can't believe this is happening."

ARTHUR: "Can anyone join Frank?"

SUE: "I can. I can't believe this is happening either. I'm trying to hold it together. Being on Zoom is reinforcing how serious the pandemic is."

The group energy cascaded into members acknowledging how scared and overwhelmed they felt. There was a subgroup of members who went numb, reporting their experience by explaining their experience.

LOU: "I want to stay numb right now."

ARTHUR: "Who else in the group can join Lou in wanting to stay numb? What's your experience like when you choose to stay numb? Can you take a moment and explore your experience below the numbness?"

Over time, the experience of our group meetings on the Zoom platform became grist for the mill. Frank, who learned that a common defense of his was to blame and complain, splitting off his experience of vulnerability and projecting it out into someone or something, is still in group and jokes periodically that group on Zoom still feels like being on *Hollywood Squares*.

As time passed, I started to realize that my experience working on Zoom felt very much like my experience working at my office. I would become fully involved in the group sessions. Working over the internet felt completely normal. I soon gave up my office of 33 years. During the five years that I've been working on Zoom, only one patient left therapy, stating she didn't feel secure engaging in therapy over the internet. Almost all patients who were in my six groups at the time when I started working on Zoom are still in my practice.

I am aware that there are a variety of pros and cons related to facilitating group over the internet. One common complaint has been that the therapist cannot see group members' nonverbal communications as clearly as in the office. On Zoom, or another platform, you generally see the patient's face and cannot see what they are doing with the rest of their body. On the one hand, this may be true. On the other hand, it is my experience that, in general, I can see several types of patients' nonverbal expressions more clearly than I did sitting in a circle in my office. I now have all group members' faces in front of me.

It is noticeable when a patient is distracted, looking down or away from the camera. I notice when a patient is nodding their head in agreement with a group-mate or sending a signal of disapproval. I may see changes in the expressions of the patient's eyes that I can now explore. At the office, sitting in a circle, I would frequently miss the nonverbal signals of group members sitting next to me. Other complaints center on a lack of intimacy and safety when working over the internet. I can understand this to be a subjective experience that should be respected.

One major benefit of working on the internet is that group members' attendance is much steadier, since they don't have to travel to my office. Members typically log on to their Zoom meeting from their homes and the offices where they work. Frequently, they will join group while on vacation. I've had groups where members dialed in from Chile, Italy, and Morocco during one session. I believe this adds to the sense of cohesion that is the glue of a group.

Working on Zoom, on the whole, has been a very positive experience for me. For therapists and patients who are open to this way of working, my experience has shown me that it can provide an effective therapeutic environment for the group process.

Fees, Payments, and Other Practicalities

During the 30-plus years I practiced in my office, my policy was to have my patients pay for each session at the beginning of each session. Patients would joke with me on occasion, saying they wrote more checks to me than anyone else. Utilizing telehealth processes changed all that.

I quickly was introduced to the world of peer-to-peer payments over the internet. At first, I was quite concerned about the safety and reliability of this new way of handling fees. I found one that was offered by a consortium of banks called Zelle, which has proven to be very reliable. I changed my policy of having patients pay each week to one of settling the balance for the month, in advance, by the 10th of each month.

I adapted my practice to this new world of technology by establishing a pattern of sending my patients a monthly email I titled my *Practice Update*. In it I would remind them of practical matters regarding my current fees, reminders to settle balances by the 10th of each month, as well as clarify vacation schedules. The concerns I had about integrating technology into my practice lessened over time. I have, on balance, come to appreciate what it has to offer.

Chapter 9

Preparing the Patient for Group

The Parallel Process in the Here-and-Now Experience

Before a patient starts the first group, I spend an individual session on what to expect. I begin by describing the group as focused on the *here-and-now experience* (Yalom & Leszcz, 2005).

> "In group we focus on the here and now. What does this mean? It means we try to pay attention to how we are impacted, as well as how we are impacting each other in the moment. The goal of the group experience is to explore our participation in relationships that unfold in the present. By staying in the present, we learn how we are actually relating to the world. By observing the here and now, we also have the opportunity to see how we tend to recapitulate old roles that were once functional but are no longer functional in our present context. Group, over time, becomes a reflection, a mirror of the way we live our lives on the outside. What we tend to do out there, we generally end up doing here."

I explain that what we see, over time, is that patients will pepper the air with parts of themselves that will inevitably induce feelings in other group members. This *in vivo* process will recreate interpersonal patterns and responses that occur outside of the group that the patient may or may not be aware of. We call this the *parallel process*. In exploring these patterns, the patient has the opportunity to become aware of how he contributes to problems that he is complaining about. He now has the opportunity to learn how to approach familiar internal and interpersonal challenges in a more effective way. He also has a choice to continue to do what he always does.

Group Norms and Agreements

Over the years, I have experienced, witnessed, and learned of different group norms adopted by a variety of very effective and established group practitioners (Yalom & Leszcz, 2005). The following are norms that I present to

DOI: 10.4324/9781003649632-9

new group patients. I have had many patients initially reluctantly comply with these norms and eventually share with the group how they came to appreciate these basic guidelines as providing safety and structure to their group experience.

Agreement To Say Everything

I clarify that an important part of our group agreement is to say everything. I will say:

> "If you're aware that something is in the way of telling us what you're experiencing, our agreement is to let me and the group know that there's something that you're aware of that you're reluctant to reveal. We now have an opportunity to explore why you're hesitant about sharing it with the group. It's more important for our work to find out what's preventing you from revealing your experience than what it is that you're not revealing. We're more interested in *why* you're holding something back than *what* you're holding back. Does that make sense?"

Generally, when the patient explores the restraining forces holding them back from revealing the content, it is not long afterward that they reveal what they were holding back (Greenson, 1967).

No Contact Outside the Group Meeting and Not Revealing Last Names

I have found that establishing the norm of not having contact outside of the group meeting has been invaluable. This norm, which I adopted from a mentor of mine, has been very helpful in preventing subgrouping. It reinforces the experience of the group being unique and special. There is no experience like it.

What also adds to its uniqueness, as well as confidentiality, is that I ask members not to reveal their last names. I ask group members not to talk to others, outside the group, about their group experience except in an abstract way. I ask group members not to mention any identifying details regarding other members in the group. We are invested in keeping the group experience confidential, even if we can't enforce it. I have patients report that even after years of knowing each other intimately it is reassuring that we don't contact each other outside of the group and do not know each other's last names.

These norms, over time, have been acknowledged to aid in members feeling safe. They reinforce that we are in a mutual project together. I try to find a balance in the group between feeling safe and not feeling too comfortable. Not having outside contact reinforces the perspective of participant/observer and not taking feedback personally.

Importance of Not Taking Feedback Personally

An essential group goal is to navigate challenging moments while still being interpersonally connected. This is what we are attempting to accomplish in the group, as well as in our lives. In order to learn from the group experience, we must develop a conscious split in awareness between our experiential self and our observing self. This process aids in developing a capacity to take in feedback without taking it personally.

Giving and receiving feedback in the group is at the core of our learning. It is inevitable that we will, at some point, inadvertently or deliberately, hurt, shame, or judge others, as well as feel hurt, shamed, or judged by others as we go through the group experience. Feedback stings, no matter how much emotional armor we develop or how resilient we become.

What is important is to be able not to take feedback personally (Agazarian, 1997)! Not taking feedback personally is the "oil that lubricates the group process."

Helping Patients Not to Take Feedback Personally

In general, I reiterate, all through our work, the importance of adopting a participant/observer role in our group experience. I reinforce that it is through maintaining our observer role that we are also training ourselves not to take feedback personally. It is through taking in feedback that we learn about how we affect others and how we may be contributing to the problems we are complaining about.

It is at this point I reinforce that one of the challenges of the group experience is to *develop the capacity* not to take feedback personally. Some patients believe this means that they should not feel discomfort, shame, anxiety, etc. when hearing negative feedback. I reinforce that listening to feedback that is not supportive always stings a bit. We are attempting to develop a thicker emotional skin, which is not easy to do and takes time to accomplish.

I clarify that taking the posture of the observing self creates emotional distance from our experiential self. This helps us develop the tolerance we need to absorb feedback that is difficult but necessary to hear. In order to maintain this posture, I reinforce the need for us to stay curious. Curiosity helps sustain our ability to stay in our observer role. It helps create some emotional distance from the impact of hearing feedback that is difficult to endure, tolerate, and admit to (Agazarian, 1997).

Finding Leverage in Dealing with the Secondary Gains of Dysfunctional Behavior

The group experience gives us the opportunity to discover how secondary gains can be a powerful force in resisting change (Ormont, 1992). I have found that attempting to persuade patients to give up dysfunctional, self-defeating behavior frequently develops into a battle of wills. I keep in mind that all behavior has a purpose.

Dysfunctional behavior can be understood to have been once functional and can still provide powerful secondary gains. One reason I suggest always keeping the patient's presenting complaints in mind is that during times like this, when the patient in fact chooses not to give up dysfunctional perspectives and behaviors, we can use it as leverage.

I tend at this point to ask the patient if they remember why they came into therapy in the first place. What are they working on? This intervention ties together the benefits of the secondary gains with the cost—the cost being the symptoms the patient came into therapy to work on in the first place. I wait for their answer.

At least now they can make a conscious choice about whether their symptoms are worth the secondary gains of their dysfunctional behavior. It also helps us understand the ambivalence in the choice if the patient is still choosing to be in therapy. I point this out to the patient.

Goodness of Fit

There are instances when I realize that a patient is not benefiting from group. Generally, it presents as a prolonged negative group experience or negative transference that never shifts. The patient has trouble developing an observing ego/self that prevents them from looking at their group experience at arm's length. This makes it difficult for the patient to develop an alternate perspective from the one that may be undermining them.

This happens to me more often when the patient is seeing another therapist in concurrent therapy. Sometimes splitting occurs. More often than not, I become the good object in the split and the patient's individual therapist becomes the bad. Sometimes it's the reverse. Frequently it's workable, sometimes not. Here is an example

> I once suggested to a patient, Don, that he try another type of therapy when, after several years of staying stuck and declining, we realized that he was recapitulating a role he developed in his family of origin. This role reflected his overt desire to be a reliable, dutiful group member while covertly he would numb himself to the therapy he was engaged in.
>
> In this dysfunctional role, Don dutifully attended all therapy sessions, coming on time, seemingly engaged in the group process, and promptly putting anything he learned in his therapy out of his mind as soon as he left the office. This pattern seemed to recreate a solution he developed in his family. Growing up in a very religious fundamentalist family, Don obediently submitted to his family's requirement that he attend church several times a week. He appeared present while quietly numbing himself and daydreaming in order to get through the service.

This insight, which he found very enlightening, didn't change anything for him. Don needed a great deal of individual therapy, which he claimed he couldn't afford. We mutually decided that the group was not helpful and I recommended he seek other forms of therapy with a focus on individual treatment, even if it meant going to an affordable clinic, which he was reluctant to consider.

Adding New Members

As a rule, I do not start a new group with less than four members. I limit my groups to eight members. I try to get a sense of a new member's potential fit in the group. I like a mix of genders and sexual preferences. Age is less important than the fit, for me. I have had groups with members ranging in age from 38 to 85, which worked very well for years. I will not add members when the group is in turmoil.

I may or may not tell the group that I am adding a member. I determine whether or not to tell the group I am adding a new member based on what is currently happening in the group. I will generally tell the group I am adding someone new if the group's cohesion is somewhat shaky. If the group is presently unconflicted (no current enactments, members open to feedback, a sense of cohesion exists, etc.) I frequently will not tell the members I am adding someone new, in order to stir up the pot.

The Group Contract

In preparing patients to join group, I discuss group norms and give them a variety of handouts describing the group contract and experience (Yalom & Leszcz, 2005).

First, I clarify that we only use first names, never surnames, for confidentiality reasons. We do not communicate outside of group, much less socialize. The process of the group is limited to the contact we have within the time and physical constraints of the group meeting. Of course, on occasion, there is resistance to these norms. This is sometimes evidenced by acting out and outright challenging of the norms. Sometimes it is more subtle.

> One group, upon exiting my office, would speak together loudly in the hallway outside my office, making sure I was able to hear them. Upon exploring their behavior during the next session, one group member blurted out with a smile, "We wanted to show you who was boss. But not to your face." This led to a fruitful exploration of a group member's authority issues.

I also reinforce that we are in a very special environment, where we learn about ourselves by being scientists as well as guinea pigs. We are attempting to split our experience into observing and experiential roles. I introduce the posture of not looking for the truth, which frequently leads to a dead end in our explorations. I maintain that we are attempting to understand and make sense of our subjective experience.

I suggest that we agree to say everything that is experienced in the here-and-now process of the group.

> "If you find that you're holding back something, let us know. An important aspect of our work is to explore why we aren't able to express ourselves. It is more important to understand why we won't reveal our experience [the process] than what we won't reveal [the content]."

Shame, guilt, and embarrassment are the common experiences that hold our patients back from revealing themselves and being known in group and in life. Our group contract brings these experiences out into the open to be identified, explored, and worked through.

Sample Group Contract

Here is an example of a typical group contract.

> Actively work on the issues that brought you to therapy.
> Translate your thoughts, feelings, and thoughts into words. Share your experience with the group or explore your reluctance to do so.
> Keep your focus on the here and now.
> Become aware of the parallel process in our group experience. We tend to behave in group in the same manner that we behave in the outside world. By observing our experiences in group, we can learn how we are affecting others in our lives outside of group.
> Take on the posture of being a *participant/observer*. In the *participant* role, we pay attention to our feelings and become aware of our experience. In the *observer* role, we take a step back to find a centered experience that is larger than just the moment. We stay curious and attempt to understand what we are experiencing.
> Attempt not to take feedback personally.
> Agree to say everything that comes up for you in group, without judging its importance. If you are reluctant to bring something up, let the group know. Agree to explore why or what is preventing you from bringing it in. Learning about the ways that we protect ourselves is as important as what we are reluctant to reveal.

As a member of the group, you are expected to:

> Have a private, consistent space with a computer, if attending a Zoom group. (During the last few years, I have only had groups meeting on Zoom.)

Share your reactions and observations of yourself and others while being respectful of other members.

Be present each week, come on time, and stay for the entire session.

Notify the group in advance of plans to be absent from a session. Tell the group why you will miss coming.

Protect the names and identities of other members in the group.

Not talk about group outside of group except in the abstract, and never use group members' names.

Not come to group having indulged in a substance.

Be financially responsible for all group meetings.

Chapter 10

Establishing a Group Therapy Culture

As I mentioned previously, early on in the process I introduce the concepts of the *observing self* as contrasted with the *experiential self*. This deliberate split in experience and perspective can help the patient develop the ability to not take in feedback personally, which then can be used to develop the *therapeutic alliance*. The therapeutic alliance can be understood to be an alliance between the patient's observing self and the therapist's *therapeutic perspective* (Greenson, 1967).

This alliance is very different from a positive transference. The therapeutic alliance requires that the patient has the capacity to look at himself without resorting to the full array of defenses we all hold onto in protecting ourselves from real and imagined threats. We cannot build a therapeutic alliance until we help the patient develop an ability to be larger than their experience, larger than the moment.

I attempt to help patients recognize the value of taking a step back and looking at themselves. I remind them of how important it is not to take feedback personally. When a patient is challenged or goes into a dysfunctional role, a positive transference can very quickly turn into a negative transference. It is at these times that I can rely on the therapeutic alliance. The therapeutic alliance is our leverage when we are challenged to reflect back something that might be difficult for the patient to accept or even be open to considering.

Developing *mutual assumptions* is key to building therapeutic alliance. Mutual assumptions emerge from being able to point out and have the patient accept that they tend to defend themselves in a particular way when feeling uncomfortable, overwhelmed, vulnerable, frustrated, etc. For it to be mutual, the patient has to acknowledge that what the therapist is proposing makes sense to them and to see that the behavior is ultimately self-defeating.

Useful Interventions in Developing a Group Culture

Developing the observing self:

"How are we doing today?"

"What is your experience like when you go silent?"

DOI: 10.4324/9781003649632-10

"I have a hunch about what is going on."

"Are you open to a different way of understanding and approaching this familiar dilemma? Are you open to trying it out with the group?"

"What was it like for you to try to relate to this situation in a different way?"

"Can I consult with the group?"

"How am I doing with Joe today?"

"How is Joe doing today?"

Increasing awareness of defenses:

"Did you notice that your voice became louder when you responded to Riley?"

"Can we slow down for a moment and see what just happened?"

"Susan told you that your manner of speaking intellectually turns her off. It seems that your solution is to stop talking. Did you notice this? What was your experience like when she said what she said?"

"Do you remember what you told me when you first sought therapy? You shared with me that you don't tend to stand up for yourself when challenged. I think it's happening right now. Let's explore what is preventing you from responding to what Riley just said to you. Can anyone join Jack in having the tendency to avoid standing up for yourself in these situations?"

Being larger than the moment:

"Remember that in order to do this work together, we'll need to develop the capacity to be larger than the moment. This allows us to increase our ability to observe ourselves in our experience and not just be in the experience. Can you let yourself focus and be curious about what is happening to you right now?"

"Do you remember that a major challenge and goal in group is developing the capacity to split our attention between the observing part of us and the experiential part of us?"

"Can we take a moment to observe your experience? What is your experience like?"

Challenging Moments: Using a Group-as-a-Whole Perspective

I have found the following group-as-a-whole interventions to be helpful in regulating moments of intense upset in group (Agazarian, 1997). I attempt to shift the focus from the heart (experiential self) to the head (observing self). I want to keep this in mind as the group finds a balance between affective and cognitive awareness.

> "It seems that you are having a difficult experience right now. Perhaps this is not just your experience. Sometimes, in group, one person can hold feelings for another or even be a voice for the whole group. Does this make sense?"

> "Does anyone resonate with Bill's anger/sadness/confusion/grief, etc.?"

> "Anybody else?" (Asking this question helps to connect members to each other and recognize they are part of a larger group process.)

> "What is happening in our group right now?"

> "What is the goal for the group at this moment?"

> "What is your goal right now?"

> "It seems that it's more important for the group to fight right now than be curious about what is being said."

> "Who is in the subgroup that's inclined to fight, and who's in the subgroup that is inclined to watch others fight?"

> "Where did we learn to do what we are inclined to do in these moments?"

> "If we were to take a step back and be observers of the group for a moment, what would we see happening in the group right now?"

Framing an Experience

Patients often feel overwhelmed by emotions, thoughts, reactions, mind reads, etc. I find it helpful to label these experiences. One example is using the familiar frame of the patient feeling "flooded." Simply labeling this for the patient frequently has a calming effect. I ask patients to slow down and be mindful of their experience.

> "Where in your body do you feel your [anger, anxiety, sadness, being overwhelmed]?"

Ambivalence Framed as Competing Parts of the Patient

> "It seems to me that you're experiencing several parts of you that are competing with each other. One part of you wants to speak to Brian another part of you is holding you back."

> "Can we explore the part that is holding you back from speaking to Brian?"
> "What about the part that wants to speak to Brian?"

Helping Patients Shift Their Communication Pattern from Explaining to Relating Effectively: Using Agazarian's "Explain vs. Explore"

Patients tend to explain a great deal about their situation. Explaining, of course, is productive when it adds to our understanding of the patient's experience. When explaining is defensive, however, the communication can become repetitive, redundant, obvious, and empty.

Frequently, explaining takes the form of a flood of words that doesn't add much to what a patient is attempting to communicate. This can be understood to be a defense that insulates the patient from experiencing underlying feelings that range from uncomfortable to intolerable (Agazarian, 1997). I find that explaining frequently takes the following forms:

Patient looks up or looks down while they speak. They avoid eye contact.
Rapid speech. Run-on sentences.
Repeating themselves.
Patient speaks in a monotone.
Patient speaks in *non sequiturs*.

When a patient is explaining, I will first point out the behavioral signals that they are presenting and ask if they notice that while they are speaking they look at the ceiling, at the floor, they aren't behind their eyes, speak without feeling, etc. A common self-defeating pattern of communication is telling the story of a traumatic experience and not relating to or through their experience.

I have worked with many patients who are in Alcoholics Anonymous (AA). I learned from these patients that this split-off style of relating traumatic experience is actually called a "war story" in AA meetings (Alcoholics Anonymous, 2001). The details might be dramatic, but the experience of listening to the details without corresponding affect frequently leaves the listener bored and empty.

It is not uncommon that when patients, in group, open up and share overwhelming personal information in a defensive manner, frequently without affect, they are disappointed by the lack of response from their groupmates. There are, of course, many individual reactions that might help us understand why members may not respond to a group member's opening up and sharing painful experiences. It is, however, curious when there is no reaction at all by any of the members to the opening up of difficult material.

When this occurs, I will ask the group, "What is our experience in the silence? Why did we become so quiet after Dave opened up about ...?" Frequently, the exploration would relate to how they became distracted, sleepy, unfocused, etc. while Dave was "telling us what happened to him."

As we explore further, we recognize that Dave's opening up about very painful material was experienced by his groupmates as being told to them with flat affect, in his describing many details that were unnecessary and repetitive. Members explore what was below their sleepiness, numbness, etc. and find that Dave's manner of explaining his story induces numbing in themselves. This gives them the excuse to ward off their own powerful feelings that resonate with and relate to Dave's experience.

When a patient seems to be struggling to communicate what they want to reveal, I tend to bring up the notion that they may be more interpersonally effective by exploring their experience rather than explaining their experience. Patients generally don't understand this at first but very much appreciate the distinction over time.

One way to address defensive explaining can be to ask patients to explore their experience below the explaining, below the words.

ARTHUR: "What is your experience below telling us about the fight with your lover?"

DAVE: "What do you mean?"

ARTHUR: "Try to explore your experience below your words describing the fight."

DAVE: "I feel a deep sense of despair. I feel sick to my stomach."

ARTHUR: "Can you take a moment and explore inside the sick feeling in your stomach?"

DAVE: "I feel very isolated, alone, and hopeless."

ARTHUR: "Can anyone resonate with what Dave is experiencing."

Our goal is to explore our experience, not explain it.

Helping Patients Move from Intellectualization

I regularly ask group members to pay attention to their experience as the session proceeds. I attempt to elicit patients' reactions to what is happening in the group (e.g., "What's your experience of everyone being silent for so long?" "What's your experience of the tension between Seth and Jill?"). Many patients I work with, early in their therapy, are frustrated by the responses they are met with when speaking in group. Frequently, it is a result of their tendency to explain their experience in an intellectualized, split-off manner.

I attempt to point this out gently. I generally compliment them on how they have a facility with words. I then ask them what their goal is in saying what they are saying. At first, they are frequently surprised by this question. They usually don't understand why I am asking this. Many have never thought about what their goal is in saying something.

I suggest that language can be used in different ways. It can be used to draw people in, to keep others at arm's length, or to keep yourself split off from your own feelings and experience. I ask patients if they can try to notice what they are feeling in their bodies as they speak. I ask them to notice what the sensation is, if any, in their eyes, throat, arms, etc. I sometimes quote Agazarian, saying "It seems your body knows something that you don't know" (Agazarian, 1997).

Over time, my patients generally become increasingly aware of how their intellectual communication, when used in a context that requires emotion, leaves them feeling frustrated, alone, isolated, impotent, or ineffective. I suggest that they reserve their tendency to use their intellectual gifts for the appropriate contexts, such as work, not intimacy. I find that this approach helps many patients become more aware of what they are saying, why they are saying it, and how it is being received.

It is during these group moments that I may bring in the notion that all behavior has a purpose. I try to get them curious about what they are experiencing internally while they are speaking. I ask them to pay attention to how they are affecting others and why others are responding to them in a particular way. This exploration can help them better understand why they are not getting the responses they hope for or expect to receive when they finally are revealing difficult emotional experiences.

Helping Patients Identify Their Feelings

ARTHUR: "In our work, you can't 'feel like' anything. You can feel or you can think. What do you feel right now?"
PATIENT: "I feel that … ."
ARTHUR: "In our work you can't 'feel like' or 'feel that' anything. Take your time and notice what is coming up for you in your body, not in your thoughts.
PATIENT: "I feel tension in my body."
ARTHUR: "Can you keep going and notice what your experience is like in your tension?"
PATIENT: "I feel burning in my eyes."
ARTHUR: "OK. So if you looked into your burning eyes what would you see?"
PATIENT: "Sadness."
ARTHUR: "Yes, I can see the sadness in your eyes."
PATIENT: "I feel sad."
ARTHUR: "Yes. Can you let yourself experience your sadness and let your sadness be as big as it has to be?"

Dysfunctional Roles that Emerge in Group

Defensive patterns of behavior that appear during the group process take on the familiar forms of projection, projective identification, cognitive distortions, flight, fight, denial, etc. One form of defense that has been particularly useful for me to recognize, identify, and work with is the development and appearance of *roles* in the group experience. I have adopted aspects of Agazarian's description of dysfunctional roles that regularly appear in the group process (Agazarian, 1997).

Dysfunctional roles, as I am using the term, reflect the *solutions* that individuals developed early in life to contend with the challenges they faced in their family of origin. These solutions are evident in the behaviors, beliefs, and attitudes the patient has imported to deal with look-alike events encountered in the present group experience. These look-alike events evoke past trauma related to failures in early dependency relationships. These solutions, or roles, generally take some form of:

Flight (laying low, staying silent, intellectualization, telling stories, asking questions, telling jokes that divert the group, etc.),
Fight (arguing, debating, talking over, quarreling, standing up and threatening to throw a chair, etc.) and/or
Fright (feeling panicky, overwhelmed, emotionally flooded, etc.)
Roles develop through a process of:

Thoughts (self-talk) that lead to feelings,
Feelings that evoke behaviors,
Behaviors that interact with the environment (other members, the therapist, or the group as a whole)
Reinforcing the thought.

Dysfunctional roles generally have a one-up/one down quality. These roles that were once functional in the context the child originally faced have now become dysfunctional. These solutions that were appropriate in their original context are no longer appropriate in the patient's present context. Inevitable anxiety and frustration emerge in the group process and are frequently experienced as a look-alike event for group members.

With its focus on the here and now, the group experience tends to stimulate the recapitulation of members' dysfunctional roles. The resulting dysfunctional roles are evidenced by the thoughts, feelings, and behaviors that emerge in group members to cope with vulnerability experienced in the group process. In group, we have the opportunity to witness how these once-useful solutions are now frequently contributing to the patient's symptoms and presenting complaints. Part of the learning in group is for group members to recognize their tendency to go into a role that frequently contributes to the problems they are working on and complaining about.

Chapter 11

Character Styles That Are Common in Group

Borderline Personality Disorder and Tendencies

The term *borderline* has been frequently used as a derogatory, throwaway description of an individual who, under stress, can be difficult and impulsive, with a tendency to act out. That description may at times be accurate (without the judgment), but I find it to be a missed opportunity to keep in mind certain dynamics when working with individuals who are organized in this manner (McWilliams, 1984).

I understand the borderline condition to describe a patient's tendency to split the world and their self-image into good and bad (Gabbard, 1994). When they or the object (person they are relating to) are experienced as good, they feel very, very good. When they or the object are bad, they feel very, very bad. The good/bad split is observed in the patient's excessive or extreme reactions to good and bad experiences in group and in their outside lives.

This tendency can be understood to reflect the patient's inability to experience the good and the bad self-image or object image at the same time. They do not remember the good when they are feeling bad. They do not remember the bad when they are feeling good.

Recognizing this tendency to split can help explain the experience of working with a patient who initially experiences you as the wisest, most empathically attuned therapist they ever had. After a challenging therapeutic moment, the therapist can suddenly be seen as incompetent, undermining, and not trustworthy. While the therapist may actually exhibit these qualities to some degree, more than likely the therapist is being viewed through the black/white, good/bad split. This tendency to split and to exaggerate the good and bad creates great challenges in these patients' relationships and within themselves.

Relationships often feel extremely good at first, for both the patient and the person they are relating to. Sooner or later, inevitable frustration emerges, which will set into motion the projection of the bad into the other person. I believe it is important to recognize these proclivities as having varying degrees of intensity, ranging from mild, to moderate, to severe. This range of intensity is frequently overlooked.

DOI: 10.4324/9781003649632-11

The therapy often focuses on their tendency to split (Kernberg, 1975). Occasionally, a patient will abortively complain, "You're not helping me." My response, after exploring the complaint when it has no solution, might be, "Well, was I ever helpful?" This non-defensive intervention works well if I have developed enough of a therapeutic alliance with the patient.

If that doesn't work, I try to explore their experience in having a therapist who can be helpful at times and not helpful at others. Is there room in the relationship for both experiences? Not being defensive in exploring how I can have both good and bad qualities, at times, seems to stabilize the patient's tendency to exaggerate their reactions to these experiences.

I have found group to be helpful in diluting the powerful negative and positive transference when it inevitably shows up in intense forms. The group environment, in contrast to individual treatment, can give us a bit more leverage when we encounter the patient splitting. We can always ask others in the group what their experience is in relation to what the patient is reacting to. "Does anyone else experience me (or another group member) as being harsh, annoyed, dismissive, etc.?" We want to make sure the patient isn't alone in his experience.

Hopefully, other group members will join the patient in their experience while expressing a milder reaction. Their milder reactions may support the content of the patient's reaction while having an experience that is less intense. This can then be an opportunity for the patient to explore and work through an intense negative transference or overreaction to a situation involving another group member or the group as a whole rather than simply acting it out.

Splitting

In my practice, I have learned the importance of spotting the tendency to split the world or oneself into good or bad (Kernberg, 1975). As I mentioned in the previous section, the giveaway to me is exaggerated reports of the patient's self-experience or descriptions of others (or the world in general) as being all good or all bad.

I have noticed an early example of the tendency to split occurs when a patient comes in for a consultation and raves about how I helped the person who referred them. Whatever I say is met with responses that leave me feeling that I'm being elevated and met with a very high expectation of competence that I have not yet and may never earn.

If we decide to work together, I ask the patient about their experience during the consultation. Patients who tend to split will comment on how they are sure I can help them, how much they like my style (as compared to their last therapist), how impressed they are with my office (when I had one), etc.

My intervention, when faced with the good fortune of being the good object in the split, is to say something like, "Thanks for the feedback. I just want to make a note of your very positive opinion of me and my work and put it in my back pocket." They will usually ask, "What do you mean?" I suggest, "At some point, when the work is very challenging, you may not feel so admiring. When that happens, I'll remind you of the things you said today." Their typical response is, "You're so modest I can't see that happening." My usual reply is, "Let's see what happens."

Bipolar Symptoms and Borderline Tendencies

I have often noticed borderline tendencies in patients who have been diagnosed as bipolar.

Bipolar symptoms are generally treated with medication, with good results. I have had some very positive outcomes treating bipolar patients clinically, in conjunction with medication prescribed by a psychopharmacologist.

The therapy focuses on becoming familiar with and not judging the individual's reactions to stress. The group experience lends itself well to helping the patient develop coping strategies in the face of emotional challenges that could be experienced as overwhelmingly bad or good.

In group, I attempt to help patients pay attention to their experience when they have an out-of-proportion experience of feeling good. Frequently, they will notice that their speech becomes pressured, and their thoughts are racing. I will try to help the patient slow down and explore their experience. I try to engage their observing self.

"What is your experience like when your thoughts are all over the place?"

"What is your experience like when you feel like you can't settle down?"

Other group members can be helpful in mirroring how the patient is affecting them. It is also helpful when other members can join the patient in having similar experiences that are distracting and not easy to regulate. We find that this swing up inevitably leads them to the exaggerated opposite experience of feeling bad or down when feeling frustration, disappointment, etc. This swing down can lead to a depressive episode.

I have found helping patients become familiar with and subsequently able to regulate their intense reactions to positive and negative experiences has helped stabilize much of their tendency toward emotional swings. I suggest to these patients that a major goal for us is to help them *self-regulate*. Many patients seem to appreciate this framing, as it lends itself to helping the patient understand how their condition can be addressed in the group environment.

Narcissistic Personality Disorder and Tendencies

In contrast to how I understand borderline features as struggling with the tendency to split the world into good and bad, which I conceptualize as a horizontal split, I find it helpful to think about narcissistic features as having a split that is vertical (one up/one down). Patients with narcissistic features frequently present with one or more of these constellations of complaints (Gabbard, 1994):

An enduring self-experience of emptiness, as contrasted to the borderline's being "filled" with anger.

Experiences of shame, inferiority, envy, numbness, or incompleteness.

Other patients present with compensatory defenses against these experiences. They may present being hypervigilant, self-righteous, victimized, superior, vain, and defensively self-sufficient. I always keep in mind that these features present on a continuum from mild, to moderate, to severe.

Patients presenting with either set of qualities, or a mix of both, have an underlying shakiness of self that is very delicate. They cannot tolerate much challenge to their fragile self-esteem. They generally have great difficulty acknowledging their "nickel in the dime" and frequently cannot take in feedback that is not very gently framed.

Individuals with narcissistic tendencies tend to struggle with internal adaptive processes that alternate between idealization and devaluation. The split appears to contribute to an experience of being one-up or one-down. They tend to view themselves or the person being related to as elevated or diminished.

I keep in mind the literature that suggests that, as a child, the individual was generally related to as an extension of the parent or caretaker. The child was experienced and used as a "utility" in the service of the parent's needs (Miller, 1997). It has been helpful to me to keep in mind that these individuals relate to intimate relationships as potential "self-objects" (Bacal, 1985).

Self-objects can be understood to be others who will validate the patient with affirmation, admiration, and approval. Once a person is no longer useful to them, they can easily leave the relationship (e.g., a lover, friend, therapist). The person to a large extent is experienced as a utility, not an attachment.

It is not uncommon to find that the patient grew up in an atmosphere of constant evaluation. The irony for many is that, even if the child is often praised, they tend to have an underlying experience of being constantly monitored and evaluated for their achievements. They feel a constant need to excel. "Where are the other eight points?" the child's father asks, only half-kidding, when she gets a 92 on an exam. It becomes ego-syntonic.

This experience frequently leaves the child with what is understood as *perfectionistic strivings*. They have unrealistic expectations of themselves that lead to either *attainment*, which supports their grandiosity, or *failure*, leading to the experience of being diminished and, often, depression. Being "good enough" is not an option.

These people are frequently successful in their professional lives but never feel a sustained sense of having achieved enough. Their accomplishments generally provide only transient moments of self-esteem. There is often a never-ending impulse to go on to the next achievement, which, even if attained, soon leaves them with the same sense of emptiness.

Individuals with narcissistic features seem to have a stunted capacity to attach and to love. Their need for others is deep but their experience of love for others is quite shallow and limited. This can be misunderstood by others, who feel they are desired and loved by the individual.

Narcissistic qualities that stand out in the group experience are a patient's general lack of remorse or gratitude. This lack seems to be an outgrowth of the patient's tendency to treat people as self-objects, as well as being trapped by their perfectionistic strivings. As a consequence of the tendency toward perfectionistic strivings, the patient has difficulty admitting a mistake. The lack of gratitude can be understood as an outgrowth of disowning the need for others. If you don't need others, you don't have to be grateful if they do something for you.

A frequent scenario related to asking for help occurs between friends, within a couple, and in group. One partner (with narcissistic features) signals that they have a need by complaining, describing a problem, wishing for something, etc. (e.g., "I'm having trouble with ... ."). They tend to ask for help or advice indirectly. The friend, partner, or in our case groupmate responds to that signal by doing something. They go out of their way to help.

In group, this takes the form of inquiring how the patient is doing and the group spending time on that particular patient's problems. The person bene-fiting from the help doesn't show gratitude. The group as a whole (or a par-ticular groupmate) frequently feels resentful or taken for granted. The individual who was helped typically responds, "I never asked you for your help." And they didn't, not directly.

I have found the group experience to be extremely helpful in being able to recognize narcissistic qualities in patients that were not so obvious in individual work. When the focus of a problem is on someone else in group or a situation outside of the patient, the therapy can proceed with a sense of success.

When asking the patient to examine their "nickel in the dime," their con-tribution to their problem, I have found they will frequently become upset and angry. This experience can be felt as a threat to their fragile self-esteem. Now they see the therapy as "lacking," they don't feel understood, "it's run its course." I am then reminded that I am a self-object. I am there as a utility to preserve their self-esteem, not challenge them.

Being able to recognize patients who have narcissistic features has helped me become more empathically attuned and to adjust the way I work with this particular type of patient. I keep this in mind, being careful not to challenge this patient directly. Instead, I may ask if others can "join" the patient. I can gently help the patient recognize how they were originally treated and used as a utility in their family of origin, and how they may not be realizing that they are relating to others in the group in the same way. I can point out how they may be unintentionally doing to others in the group what was done to them in the family.

Confusing a Narcissist's Need for Love with Love for the Patient

"My father always wants me to visit him. He keeps saying that he wants to see me. He must love me. However, whenever I do have contact with him, I always feel empty, upset and depressed afterwards. What is wrong with me?" The narcissist's need for love is deep. Their ability to love is shallow (Gabbard, 1994).

I have had patients become very frustrated and confused in relationships where they repeatedly feel needed and wanted by someone they value and inevitably feeling disappointed by that person, or worse. This issue appears in group when a member presents a need. This is often in the form of a problem. Members frequently become invested in "helping" this patient but ultimately end up feeling empty, disappointed, upset, and angry.

> An example of this occurred recently in group when Sam, who tended to keep relationships at arm's length, received a great deal of attention in several groups when he opened up as to how he felt "stuck" in his four-year relationship. His significant other was starting to pressure him to get married, and he was becoming very uncomfortable with her and within himself. He didn't want to lose her, but he couldn't bring himself to commit to marrying her.
>
> His groupmates, encouraged by his finally showing vulnerability, enthusiastically joined him in acknowledging how they, as a result of their own fear, could also keep relationships and themselves stuck. Much energy was focused on Sam's and the group's experiences of feeling stuck. The group as a whole commented on how open and available Sam appeared to be. There seemed to be progress being made in his acknowledging to the group and himself how he was adversely affecting his girlfriend, who wanted more commitment.
>
> His previous stance was generally a cold, defensive, "She's a big girl, she can take care of herself" attitude. Several of his groupmates again joined him and volunteered how they too could keep important relationships at arm's length. The refrain was basically, "I can't commit, I can't let go." Several members commented that Sam seemed to be more fully a part of the group. There seemed to be an increased sense of cohesiveness. This occurred during the last group session before my summer break.
>
> When sessions resumed after the break, Sam was the only member who didn't show up for the first two meetings. When Sam showed up for the

third meeting, Mary asked why he missed the first two groups. Sam, avoiding eye contact, vaguely commented that he had to attend to "some things." Mary asked if those other things couldn't have been attended to at another time. He didn't answer clearly. He hemmed, he hawed, he stammered, he looked up at the ceiling. Several members in the group expressed how exasperated they were with him.

Mary, who was working on issues related to trust in dependency relationships, where she generally overextended herself, exclaimed, "I'm done. You show up needing and wanting attention, but did you think for a moment that maybe you owed it to the group to show up and not blow us off?"

Sam's response mirrored Mary's. "You're done? Well, I'm done too." The group as a whole was clearly in fight, and Sam was beginning to scapegoat himself by defending himself and attacking Mary. I asked the group if we could step back and explore what was happening in the group right now.

Keeping in mind the notion that the narcissist's need for love is deep while their ability to love is shallow, I was able to have the group explore their intense reactions to Sam as well as his own surprise that they would make a big deal about it.

Witnessing a Rupture and Repair in Group

Continuing the example above:

Sam stayed silent as his groupmates explored having experienced relationships with individuals in their lives that paralleled what was occurring in the group. They explored feeling being taken for granted. Some admitted that they had been guilty of doing the same thing.

Sam explored and admitted that sometimes he could be very cold and experience others as being "not fully real to me. I don't think about what they feel except in a vague, intellectual way. I don't believe I really matter, anyway." Sam admitted that he was surprised at Mary's reaction to his not showing up for the group meetings. "It never occurred to me that anyone would really care."

As we continued our exploration, Mary and Sam started to repair their ruptured relationship. They were tentatively open to hearing each other's reaction to what occurred. Gradually, both Mary and Sam experienced and demonstrated genuine remorse for their part in the fight. Mary, who had a way of bringing humor into the group, looked at Sam and said, "OK, I'm not going to divorce you anymore." This moment contributed significantly to softening the tension in the room.

This delicately unfolding process was important for everyone in the group. It was significant for both Mary and Sam, who indicated that they had rarely witnessed or been involved in a repair when they or others were upset with each other. Other group members voiced relief. Several members commented on how it was rare for them to witness or repair a rift in relationships. It was not long afterwards that Sam informed the group that he had asked his girlfriend to marry him.

By the way, Sam's presenting complaint was focused on moderate depression experienced as feeling empty, very lonely, and not feeling close to others.

Projection and Projective Identification

I sometimes find psychoeducation to be very helpful in demystifying our work with patients. With the right group, at the right moment, I might share this classic story that helps clarify what a projection might look like and how it could provoke a projective identification (Kibel, 1993).

John was taking a leisurely drive up a beautiful hilly road when, all of a sudden, he realized he had a flat tire. He went to change his tire and realized he was missing his jack. The area was sparsely populated. He spotted a house up the road and began to walk toward the house, hoping someone was home and would lend him a jack.

As he walked, he took in the beauty of the scenery and was feeling wonderful. He smiled and thought, "What a great day, I'll just walk up that hill and maybe I'll meet some nice people who will be generous and happy to help." These thoughts put him in a pleasant mood.

Continuing up the hill, he started getting winded and tired; his mood began to shift, he felt irritated. His thoughts began to mirror his mood, "Boy, I'm out of shape. This hill is steeper than I thought. I hope there's someone home in that house."

He continued walking, feeling increasingly tired and irritated. His thoughts started to cascade into more negative scenarios. "What if no one's home? What if they don't have a jack? What if someone is home and they're afraid of strangers and won't lend me their jack? These isolated people always seem to be paranoid. These isolated people are pretty weird. You know, I wouldn't be surprised if they're home, unfriendly, paranoid, and won't lend me their jack even if they have one!"

At that point, flooded by all these negative thoughts prompting his discomfort and agitation, he reached the house and knocked on the door. A man opened the door and said, "Hello, how can I help you?" John, gripped by his fatigue, bad mood, and negative predictions, looked at him and out of breath blurted out, "Fuck you, and fuck your jack."

This snapshot gives us an example of several important processes that we commonly encounter in group and in life outside the group. First, I help patients recognize that feelings may come from different sources. They can be a reflection of their actual experience. They can also simply be a reflection of thoughts.

John's uncomfortable physical experience led to negative thoughts that contributed to his becoming increasingly agitated. These thoughts could be understood to induce a bad internal experience that he was containing. This internal experience can be *projected* onto another person.

Projection can be understood as experiencing uncomfortable emotions and attributing (projecting) them onto someone else. John believes, based on his internal experience and thoughts, that the other person has certain qualities. In this case, John projected his bad feelings and thoughts onto the person who in his mind was going to be unfriendly, paranoid, and withholding.

If the projection induces the person, in this case John, to behave in a way that provokes the other person, it can be understood to be an instance of what we call a *projective identification*. John's behavior in exclaiming, "Fuck you …" most likely would "land" in the homeowner, causing him to become hostile toward John. John could then believe that his negative thoughts about the homeowner being unfriendly and paranoid were correct. John doesn't take into account that it was his thoughts and resultant behaviors that induced the homeowner to become aggressive toward him.

The badness (the bad feeling) in John is projected by provocative behavior into the homeowner. The homeowner becomes provoked, giving the bad feeling a home, and behaves in a reciprocal way. In this case, the homeowner may have slammed the door in John's face as a result of John's aggression.

This self-fulfilling prophecy then convinces John that he was ultimately correct ("I was right! These people are mean-spirited, paranoid, unfriendly, and would have never lent me their jack."). He doesn't see his "nickel in the dime."

In group, I continually point out cognitive distortions that take the form of negative and positive predictions of the future, ruminations of the past, and assumptions of other members' internal experiences, which Agazarian called *mind reads* (Agazarian, 1997). These processes also contribute to what I understand as dysfunctional roles and role locks.

Recognizing and Addressing Dysfunctional Roles and Role Locks

Throughout the group process, I find it helpful to reinforce the importance of recognizing and becoming familiar with dysfunctional roles and role locks (Agazarian, 1997). This skill has been invaluable in my being able to help patients recognize self-defeating patterns in which they engage. (The following section on roles and role locks is an outgrowth of consultations with Yvonne Agazarian that I developed into workshops given at various conferences.)

Roles can be understood to be a constellation of:

Thoughts that lead to feelings,
Feelings that induce behaviors,
Behaviors that interact with the context,
Reinforcing the thought.

This breakdown represents the components of a type of self-fulfilling prophecy that, under stress, patients tend to import into intimate, dependency, and authority relationships. Dysfunctional roles can be understood to be the solutions that the child developed to deal with the difficulties they faced in their family of origin.

In group, members begin to recognize that the solutions they are using to deal with anxiety, frustration, threat etc. in their group experience are the same "solutions" they developed to deal with problems they faced in their early dependency relationships. They start to recognize how these "solutions" are "being unconsciously imported" and inappropriate to the current context.

What Contributes to Roles Emerging in Group?

The here-and-now focus of group highlights the miscues, misattunements, provocations, and general frustrations that patients react to by going into their familiar self-preserving roles. These roles, which were, at one point, functional solutions to problems they faced in their family of origin, are frequently dysfunctional in the current context that emerges in group and current relationships.

How Can we Recognize and Identify Roles as they Emerge in Group?

A lack of clarity, ambiguity, argumentativeness, cognitive distortions, debating, and low voice are signs of a dysfunctional role. Other qualities experienced in group are excessiveness, passion, tenacity, lack of curiosity, and overreacting. Unyielding viewpoints, perspectives, patterns of communication, and a frame of mind that is not curious signal other characteristics of roles.

What are Complementary Role Locks?

When we are in a familiar but dysfunctional role, we tend to send out cues that others in the environment respond to in a reciprocal way. This can be understood as a result of a split-off, unacceptable part of a patient that is projected (through behaviors) into the individual they are relating to. This projection induces the other person to relate to him in a manner that replicates his split off, intolerable experience (which is what may have happened to John in the above illustration).

These role locks take on a one-up/one-down pattern. Typical one-up/one-down role locks are bully/victim, rescuer/rescued, scapegoat/scapegoater, entertainer/entertained, leader/follower, etc.

An Example of a Common Complementary Role Lock

The bully, who has split off the victimized child in him/herself, cannot stand to see the vulnerability in another, as it reminds him of his own vulnerable experiences. He cannot hold back his contempt, judgment, rage, etc. toward someone he sees as weak and vulnerable, and he is compelled to act it out, either physically or verbally.

The victim, concurrently, splits off his strength and projects it into someone who appears strong and will have contempt for his own annoying, persistent weakness. He acts it out by taking the abuse and hating himself. The here-and-now experience of group permits us to recognize, identify, explore, and work on dysfunctional roles and role locks that inform the self-destructive attitudes, postures, and behaviors that tend to undermine our patients and ultimately cause them to seek treatment.

Chapter 12

Common Clinical Issues Encountered in Group

Working with Depression

Patients often inquire or challenge me as to how group can help their depression. First, I suggest that it helps to approach their depression as a symptom, not the cause of their distress. I present to them the perspective of depression as being an outgrowth of experiencing chronic helplessness and hopelessness in their lives, with resulting low self-esteem (American Psychiatric Association, 2013).

I clarify that self-esteem is directly correlated to mastery. A lack of mastery in relationships, in love, work, or both, undermines our sense of self. I introduce the distinction between *self-esteem* and *self-image*. These qualities are often believed to be the same, or interchangeable. They are not. I suggest that self-image, which is generally reinforced or undermined by external qualities (appearance, postures, strength, etc.), is quite different from self-esteem, which is related to and an outgrowth of mastery. I mention studies that found inmates in prison scoring very high on self-image but very low on self-esteem.

Framing depression as an experience of hopelessness, helplessness, and a lack of mastery that leads to shaky self-esteem helps me demystify depression and give patients some clarity as to how group can help. With the focus on interpersonal mastery and working through intrapsychic obstacles, patients can more readily understand that the manner in which they relate to others and the responses they receive have a great effect as to how they feel about themselves.

I explain that the process of focusing on the here and now provides us with an opportunity to observe ourselves in the moment. This experience contributes to their becoming more aware of how their attitudes and behaviors are affecting others in their lives in ways they do not expect or intend.

We can observe, *in vivo*, what patients are thinking and doing that brings them closer or further away from their interpersonal goals. The increased recognition and acceptance of the parallel process, which generally takes time, can help patients recognize how they are affecting others in their lives in the same manner that they are affecting others in their group experience.

I invite patients to consider the group experience to be an opportunity to take chances and make interpersonal mistakes with the goal of learning to

DOI: 10.4324/9781003649632-12

relate more effectively in their lives outside of the group. I suggest to the patient that it is through these processes that the group experience can have a positive effect on the sense of hopelessness, helplessness, and low self-esteem that underlies their depression.

Happiness Cannot Be Pursued—It Must Ensue

Many patients complain about not being happy. I have found it very useful to introduce Victor Frankl's (2006) suggestion that

> … happiness cannot be pursued: it must ensue, and it only does so as the unintended side-effect of one's dedication to a cause greater than oneself or as the by-product of one's surrender to a person other than oneself.
>
> (pp. xiv–xv)

Many patients respond to this notion by feeling relieved, having believed they were incapable of happiness. I suggest that group gives us an opportunity to discover what is truly meaningful for us. This frequently leads to an exploration of what is meaningful for the patient. Inevitably, the exploration leads to recognizing how the meaning underlying a patient's happiness or unhappiness has much to do with the quality of their attachments in life.

It follows naturally that the group experience is an opportunity to learn what are the strengths leading to and obstacles interfering with our ability to establish healthy attachments on the road to experiencing happiness.

Boredom

"I'm bored!" When someone says this, I tell the group that boredom does not exist in our group. It is a defense against experience. I ask the patient, "What is below the boredom?" This question frequently leads to "I don't know." My response of, "If you did know, what would you discover?" generally leads to the patient becoming curious about the experience that they had split off and often becoming aware of it.

I used this technique during a tense moment that occurred during a workshop I gave at a conference.

> Robert, a senior, well-regarded therapist who was in my experiential group, spoke up after a long silence, saying he was bored. I experienced that comment as a provocation, a challenge. For a moment, I stiffened. I had the momentary negative prediction that he was going to undermine this 90-minute, time-limited experiential group. I quickly quieted my growing discomfort using the aforementioned process.
>
> I suggested that in this group process boredom didn't exist. He seemed curious. I asked him what was below his boredom. He smiled. He started

to open up and acknowledge that he felt envious of others in the group, who seemed to easily relate to each other.

He revealed that he had felt left out and isolated. His boredom covered over his discomfort of not feeling connected with other group members and not being able to find a way in. I asked the group if anyone could join Robert. Several members revealed that they too felt uncomfortable, not finding a way to participate in what group members were talking about.

I suggested that we not talk about anything in the group. Our goal in this group was to explore our experience, not talk about it. This moment opened up a lively exchange among the group members that filled the balance of this time-limited group.

While we were reflecting on the group experience, I turned to Robert and asked him, "On a scale of 0 to 10, how bored are you now?" He good-naturedly replied that he appreciated the way I handled the situation. I was relieved.

It appeared that my being able to meet Robert's challenge without becoming defensive opened up a very meaningful exploration of how members in the group protected themselves from upsetting experiences by defending themselves (Yalom & Leszcz, 2005). In this case the defense was boredom.

Working with Anger

When anger is acted out in group, I attempt to shift the focus from the content of the anger to the experience that is underlying the anger. I generally try to use interventions that enable the group to take a step back and try to apprehend what is happening in the here and now, *not what has happened that led to the anger.*

Some interventions I might use are:

"Let's all take a deep breath together."

"On a scale of one to ten, what is the level of tension and upset in our group right now?"

"Let's take a moment and explore what is right below the anger you are experiencing."

"Can anyone join Ann's anger?"

"What does John's anger contain for the group?"

"What might you be avoiding by getting angry at Jill?"

"Remember, our goal is to separate out our observing self from our experiential self and not take in feedback personally."

"Who is in the subgroup of wanting to fight?"

"Who is in the subgroup of wanting to watch the fight?"

"Where did you learn to do this?"

"Can anyone join Allison?"

"What is it like to watch Jack get angry?"

"Where did you learn how to fight like that?"

"Where did you learn to lay low when you witnessed anger?"

ARTHUR: "Where's the anger residing in your body?"
PATIENT: "My throat."
ARTHUR: "Okay, take a moment to stay with your throat. Allow yourself to feel the energy in your throat. What's your experience like?"

If the energy is still too hot, I may focus on a patient's or the group's therapeutic goals.

ARTHUR: "Jill, what's your experience when Jack speaks to you like this?"
JILL: "I'm scared, hurt, and furious."
ARTHUR: "Jack, do you remember why you're here? You're here because [keeping in mind his group goal] when frustrated you have a tendency to erupt in anger. Your anger can be very intimidating and can damage relationships. What's your goal right now? Remember, our group goal is to be participant/observers in this group and not take feedback personally. So if we take a step back and explore what is happening in this moment, what do you see, what's your experience like?"

Reminding the Group to Stay in the Here and Now

Throughout the group process, I find myself reminding the group that our focus is on the here and now (Yalom & Leszcz, 2005). It is very common for members to go into storytelling or reporting in great detail about something that is going on in their lives. Too often groups focus solely on content. The content might be describing the past, storytelling, speaking about outside relationships, and becoming emotionally avoidant to what is present in the room. These processes can be understood as group defenses that dampen the emotional impact of staying in the here and now.

I have found focusing on content frequently contributes to a group that has a great deal of excitement and energy at first but slowly evolves into a group that is "dead in the water." I suggest to the group that we imagine that nothing exists outside of the group. Our sole focus should center on our experience here in the group.

> "Imagine we're forever on a small boat out in the sea. Nothing exists outside of the boat. All our attention, all of our experience, reflects what we're thinking, feeling and experiencing inside this boat with no one but our groupmates to relate to."

Using Present-Focused Language

I generally use language that is present tense, even if it sounds odd (Yalom & Leszcz, 2005). "What *is* your experience like *now* that Jane has revealed how she feels toward you?" not "What *was* your experience like when …?".

With highly intellectualized patients who slip into storytelling or outside problems at length, I might inquire, "As you share this important information, what's your experience like now below your words?" With patients who relate how they were feeling several moments ago, I ask:

ARTHUR: "What is your experience right now?"
PATIENT: "I feel like … ."
ARTHUR: "I feel like … doesn't exist in our group. You can only 'feel' a feeling."
PATIENT: "What do you mean?"
ARTHUR: "I feel has to be followed by a feeling … I feel confused, sad, lost …"

I might also ask, "If we explore below your thoughts, what do you want the group to know about you and your experience at this moment?" With patients who don't know what they feel, I may suggest that they consult with the group:

PATIENT: "But I don't know how I feel."
ARTHUR: "That's a start. Would it be helpful to have your groupmates let you know what they would feel in this moment?"

Patients Who Have Difficulty Accessing Feelings

Over the years, I have worked with many high-functioning patients who have trouble identifying what they are feeling (Ormont, 1992). I have encountered patients becoming very frustrated and anxious in not being able to answer the simple question, "What are you feeling?"

> Mark, referred by another therapist, joined one of my groups because he was stuck in his individual therapy. He could not say what he had accomplished in his therapy. I asked him what his goals were. He could not say more than vaguely "to feel less hopeless." The one feeling that was available to him was despair, which was connected to the thought, "Why try?"

We discovered that when asked what he was feeling his response was to look up, explain, and then analyze himself. This defense worked well early in his individual therapy. He enjoyed learning about himself intellectually. At first these explorations left him feeling hopeful. However, over time, the analysis "went in circles," leading to his feeling "stuck in his therapy and stuck in his life." He was at an emotional "dead end."

Early on in our work, we recognized that Mark defended himself from painful, upsetting, or vague feelings by intellectualizing and explaining what he was thinking. This observation became a mutual assumption that he gratefully held onto.

My approach was to have him agree to let me ask him, at any time during our group process, what he was experiencing and feeling, *not what he was thinking*. If he couldn't identify his experience, I would help him and I would have the group help him by giving him a multiple-choice list of what others in the group might be feeling if they were in his shoes. He liked the suggestion. He felt relieved.

In group, as was his pattern, when asked what he was feeling, he would start to explain and intellectualize. I would point out that he was using his head instead of exploring his heart. I would encourage him to focus on his experience "below his neck." He held onto that metaphor with a cheerful smile.

Patients Who Feel Nothing

Not infrequently, patients claim they feel nothing. My response that "Nature abhors a vacuum" frequently piques their interest. I attempt to bring their attention to the experience in their eyes, throat, chest, or shoulders.

ARTHUR: "Can you take a moment and notice the sensations you're experiencing in your body? Can you pay attention and notice what your body is communicating to you about your experience?"
PATIENT: "I feel a tightness in my stomach."
ARTHUR: "Good. Can you take a moment and look inside that tightness? What do you see?"
PATIENT: "Inside my stomach, I feel scared."
ARTHUR: "Good. What's scaring you?"

Chitchatting

With a group that is engaging in chitchat, I redirect group members' attention to being curious about their experience:

"What problem is the group solving by chitchatting?"

"What would the group be focused on if we weren't chitchatting?"

Not uncommonly members will answer that the last group was very disturbing, and members wanted to "lighten it up."

A Goldilocks Moment

"You're talking too much" [referring to me, the therapist]. I generally respond by thanking the member for telling me. I ask other group members what their experience was like when I was intervening.

Frequently there are two or three subgroups present, which seems to echo the Goldilocks fable. One subgroup experiences me as talking too much, one saying they want more, the third frequently saying "it was just right." I may mention that it seems we are having a Goldilocks moment. I open up an exploration of all three responses, which generally reflect what members are projecting into the group or onto me.

Harry, who had limited patience for my indulging in psychoeducation, explored how he would lose his emotion when I was "teaching the group." Harry said, "I feel lectured to, just like I did with my father."

I asked others in the group what their experience was like. Several suggested that it affected them in a similar way. Several others who tended toward intellectualization wanted even more psychoeducation. This was explored by the group to be a subjective experience, not an objective truth.

At some point, I teasingly asked the group to let me know when I was going on too long for them. Harry, the patient who brought this up in the first place, silently smiled and with his hands formed the letter T. Without a word, he communicated his need by mimicking the "time out" signal used in pro football. The group as a whole loved it. He would use this signal over the years whenever I was speaking too long and losing him.

Addressing Avoidance and Distraction

When patients seem distracted, bored, or preoccupied, I tend to reflect back what I see them doing behaviorally.

"What occurred right before you changed the subject and closed your eyes?"

"I see you looking down at the rug. What's there?"

"What do you see out the window?"

"What's your experience like when you're looking up at the ceiling?"

Chapter 13

Common Challenges in Group

Scapegoating

My understanding of *scapegoating*, the experience of accusing and/or blaming others, originated in the bible. The Hebrews, in celebrating the holiday of Yom Kippur, engaged in a ritual of slaughtering two goats. One was slaughtered to atone for the sins of the community. The other was understood to carry the sins of the community. This goat, the escape goat, carrying the sins of the community, was brought to the outskirts of the community and cast out. This action, it was believed, left the community members without sin.

Scapegoating occurs in group when a group member is seen and is related to as bad (sinful), while everyone else is good (sinless). Normally, this process is evident when a group member behaves in a way that provokes others in the group, who then see that group member as bad. Common examples include members coming in chronically late, being generally distracted, not paying attention, and engaging at inappropriate times. Agazarian (1997) called this "volunteering for the scapegoat role." The group member behaves in a way that can give others justification to accuse, judge, and blame him.

> Mike, a relatively new member, would regularly arrive 10, 12, 15 minutes late to every meeting. Every week the same process would occur, in which group members, in Mike's absence, would gripe about his being late. Interestingly, when Mike arrived, group members would abortively interrupt what had been a lively sharing of negative feelings toward him.
>
> When this process repeated itself for four or five weeks, I asked the group what was going on. Why did everyone in the group avoid addressing Mike's lateness in his presence? The exploration led to an admission by everyone that they were avoiding an uncomfortable confrontation. The group was in "flight."
>
> By the time we started to deepen our exploration of several members' avoidance experiences and how this pattern played out in their lives, Mike arrived. Again, the group went silent. I asked if we could explore the

DOI: 10.4324/9781003649632-13

silence. Someone volunteered that they were avoiding a confrontation with Mike. Others joined the "I'm avoiding" subgroup.

Mike started defending himself by explaining why he was late each week. His reasons included the subway, the elevator, a last-minute important phone call, and having to eat something. Members in the group became indignant, impatient, and frustrated.

Several started attacking Mike, saying that they too had outside pressures but they still arrived on time. "Are you kidding?" one exclaimed provocatively. The group became silent.

The underlying tension was palpable. At this point I reminded the group that it was important to take on the role of participant/observer and to remember not to take feedback personally. I said, "Let's see what we can learn from this." I asked the group to notice how there didn't seem to be anyone in the group who could relate to being late themselves. "You mean Mike is the only one in the group that comes late to things? This seems a bit curious."

A moment later, several members opened up about how, of course, they were late to things. We explored a wide range of experiences related to obligations and ambivalence related to meeting those obligations. One member even admitted that she envied Mike. She had a punishing internal voice that wouldn't permit her to dare be late.

I facilitated an exploration of how group members were splitting off their "sins" and projecting them, through their behavior, into scapegoating Mike. Members, keeping in mind the parallel process, were open to acknowledging how they were doing this, in the group as well as in their relationships outside the group.

We explored how this process undermined members' relationships. One member sadly stated that this exploration was helping her understand how she may have been contributing to some of the distance she was experiencing with her two children. She recognized that she could become exceedingly harsh and judgmental when they disappointed her by doing things she herself had done (such as shoplifting, or being defiant).

As we continued to explore everyone's experiences, I brought up how it seemed that Mike was "volunteering for the scapegoat role." This framing was surprising to hear but eagerly accepted by several members of the group, including Mike. Mike admitted that this process occurred frequently in his relationship with his lover, his relationships with authority figures at work, as well as in his family of origin. Several other members joined him in recognizing how they volunteer for this role themselves.

In exploring his experience, Mike acknowledged that there was a part of him that was communicating a "fuck you, you can't control me" sentiment in coming late. This nonverbal provocation contributed to the reciprocal aggression experienced by his groupmates. We explored how he developed this dysfunctional role. He admitted that he had the reputation of being the "bad boy" in his family of origin. He learned that negative attention was better than getting none at all from his emotionally distant, controlling, and inconsistent parents. Other group members joined him with their own subjective experiences.

This group moment was leading to and could have resulted in a very polarized outcome for the group. By framing it as the group scapegoating Mike, and exploring its implications for everyone in the group, it led to members reporting a greater sense of trust and increased risk-taking. The group seemed to have developed increased cohesion. We were able to deal with a difficult, awkward, and intimidating situation that preserved everyone in the group.

Interventions

The key is focusing on the process, not the content:

"What's our experience like when we avoid saying anything to Mike when he's late?"

"What's our experience like targeting Mike?"

"What's our experience like when we recognize we are more like Mike than we acknowledge to ourselves?"

"Does anybody else have a fuck-you side to them?"

"How do you feel toward yourself when you're the one who's late?"

Handling Enactments

Sooner or later, heated, affect-laden group moments, which can be described as *enactments*, will inevitably occur in group. Enactments stand out as group experiences imbued with intense emotions. These highly charged emotional moments can range from mild, to moderate, to severe. During enactments, many of the observations about group members' dysfunctional tendencies come alive in the group. They are fueled by cognitive distortions, projections, projective identification, roles, and role locks. Although facilitating a group during these intense moments can be challenging, I have found them to be instances where the opportunity for learning is ripe.

Alternatively, I have found that if enactments are not handled well the group as a whole can develop a tendency to go into flight. Group members start to avoid challenging interpersonal moments when they arise, or worse. The group can enter a period of being "dead in the water."

I have found that framing these occurrences as enactments can help to cool down the emotional temperature. At these times, I tend to strongly reinforce the group norms of not taking feedback personally and teasing out group members' observing selves to understand what just happened.

Interventions

"Let's take a step back and explore what just happened."

"What's our experience like in this silence?"

"Who can join Emily in her experience of not feeling safe?"

"Who can join Ruth in feeling misunderstood?"

"Can anyone join Jamie in not knowing what to say?"

Member Dropping Out Abortively

I generally ask patients about their decision to leave the group.

"When did you decide it was time for you to leave the group?"

"Why now?"

I will ask the patient if they have room to hear the group members' reactions, which can range anywhere from, "She has a right to do what she wants" to "What?" to "Can't you give us a few sessions to say goodbye?"

At some point I will ask the patient if they would like to hear my reaction to this announcement. I suggest to the patient and the group that endings in a relationship are generally difficult. They are frequently cut short because they tend to bring up great discomfort or are look-alike events related to important losses in the patient's and group members' lives.

I then support the patient's right and responsibility to themselves and the group in determining the way they want to say goodbye. However, I do recommend that we go through a process of termination (Yalom & Leszcz, 2005). I clarify that termination is a process that attempts to explore the patient's ending in a meaningful way. It can contribute to bringing closure to an important experience in the patient's life.

Patients often change their mind during this process, which is frequently the result of expressing uncomfortable feelings that have been withheld. These feelings can be directed toward me, another member, or the whole group. Sometimes patients feel freer to reveal these unexpressed feelings when there is nothing to lose because they are leaving.

I am very careful not to have the patient feel accused of running away from important issues. I have seen this communication have a very undermining effect on group cohesion, where patients fear they will never be able to leave because "there is always something to work on." More often than not, the patient leaves. I try to help the patient leave with dignity, having gone through a goodbye that was thoughtful, supportive, and hopefully meaningful.

Introducing the idea of a termination process has been consistently very helpful for individual members and the group as a whole in witnessing the end of a relationship that is not polarized and aborted. I generally recommend that the patient remain for a few sessions to reflect on what leaving the group means to them at this time. It also gives them and their groupmates a little time to absorb the decision and say goodbye. This process is not always easy.

I ask patients to consider if they reached their goals in therapy. If not, why not? If they believe they reached their goals, do the others in the group recognize the changes in the patient? If they haven't reached their goals, how are they going to work on them? Another type of therapy?

One patient told the group he was going to invest in a weekend of therapy utilizing the microdosing of hallucinogens. He said, "This type of therapy was too slow and painful." I asked this patient if he could contact me in the future and let me know if it was helpful.

I suggest that patients reflect on what was helpful in this therapy and what was not. I propose that most patients who have been in the group for a while give termination four weeks, more or less, depending on what emerges.

The Silent Group

When there appears to be a dynamic that seems avoidant, such as extended silences, I generally will think in terms of group-as-a-whole interventions. In this case, I keep in mind Bion's basic assumption groups and recognize that the group seems to be in flight. I find it very helpful to frame it in these terms because it helps create a roadmap for understanding the dynamic in front of me and how to approach it.

Assuming the group is in flight leads me to questions regarding what the group as a whole might be avoiding. First, I consider what was happening in the group right before the extended silence. Frequently, the silence is an attempt to ward off intense, intolerable emotion, both good and bad.

Sometimes the silence may communicate a moment shared and "digested" by the group that did not require words (e.g., an emotional repair between two members).

"What's your experience like in the silence?"

"What was your experience like before you went silent?"

"What might the group be avoiding by being quiet for such an extended period of time?"

I have been surprised, at times, to find that the silence was not an avoidance at all, but just the opposite. Sometimes it has been an attempt to hold onto an experience that was deeply felt, such as sadness, feeling moved, surprise, or having an "aha moment."

Making a Group Member the Identified Patient

My introduction to group therapy was one in which group members would take turns bringing in problems. One group member, for a period of time, would become the center of the group's attention. Other members would react to the member's problems in terms of how they were being affected by the content or the process of the group member's presentation.

For example, a member would comment on how Mark presented his problem. "Mark goes on so long, is not clear, and is always complaining and blaming someone else." This would lead to a lot of questions and subsequent analysis about the group member's issues and current life situation. "Mark seems to blame and complain when he is frustrated. That really turns me off. If he's doing this with his wife, it's no wonder she reacts that way."

Patients referred to this experience as "being in the hot seat." In general, this process was seen as helping members understand more about themselves and then giving them an opportunity to relate more effectively in group and in their lives. It was understood that by witnessing someone else work on their problems, other group members could learn something about themselves without the pressure of being focused on.

What generally happened over time is that the group would tend to split into subgroups. One subgroup would enjoy being the focus and would regularly bring in issues. The other subgroup would analyze the identified patient (Agazarian, 1997), asking a lot of questions, giving feedback, and avoiding the hot seat.

These processes were taken for granted and never explored. Over time, the group energy would become redundant and stall. Issues in the here and now were avoided in order to avoid being put in the hot seat. The group would either be in flight or a few patients would monopolize the group with their issues. Another subtle outcome of making members the identified patient is the tendency to intellectualize and remain engaged in a split-off group experience of analyzing each other.

I have found that moving away from a focus on an identified patient to one in which the energy is centered on exploring the here and now in the group leads to generating heightened interpersonal experiences that can result in an evolving and meaningful group culture. But not focusing on an identified patient doesn't mean that members are not encouraged to bring in their problems. Members bring in their problems, but the focus is not on the exploration of the problem and how to approach it. Group members are encouraged to relate to the issues brought up and join members who are struggling with an issue.

Working in the here and now, while also keeping in mind the patient's goals, allows for the development of themes that address the issues that brought members to group in the first place. I have found that focusing on a patient's roles, tendencies toward role locks, interpersonal styles, nonverbal signals, cognitive distortions, destructive self-talk, ineffective interpersonal attempts at intimacy, etc. has been a very productive alternative to working on a "round-robin" of alternating identified patients.

Interventions

Use curiosity to break the focus on an identified patient:

> "What's our experience when we keep asking Les these questions?"

> "What's your experience when you're the focus of the group's attention?"

> "What's your experience when you can't get the group's attention?"

Encourage joining:

> "Can anyone relate to Alex's difficulties?"

> "Is Brad the only one who procrastinates?"

> "Can anyone join Fran's laying low?"

> "What's your experience listening to Mia complain about her partner?"

Dysregulated Patients

Inevitably, over the course of our work, which can be quite challenging at times, patients will occasionally become dysregulated. When this occurs, I do the opposite of what I normally do. I attempt to move the focus of their attention away from their experience and toward their head. I encourage group members to join the dysregulated member in order to counter the common experience of being alone and exposed.

> "Ed, can you take a step back and find your curiosity?"

> "Can anyone relate to Ellie's experience?"

> "Who can join Vera in feeling completely fed up?"

If no one joins the dysregulated member, I will join on process, not content. I may use language that tones the energy down a bit without losing the sentiment of what is being said.

PATIENT: "I can't take this bullshit anymore!"

ARTHUR: "Yes, I can certainly resonate with you in having experienced moments where I couldn't stand it anymore."

ARTHUR: "I see how upset you are right now. Can you take a moment and try to settle a bit?"

PATIENT: "No."

ARTHUR: "Okay, how about if we all take a moment so the whole group can settle together?"

PATIENT: "OK, I'll try."

As the heat in the room dies down, I gently remind the group that part of our work is to develop emotional resilience and to increase our frustration tolerance. This requires that we learn to tolerate shame, guilt, and embarrassment, which is not easy. I remind them that in our group experience, "It's all grist for the mill."

Addressing the Protest of "Blaming the Victim"

Shame, guilt, and embarrassment are commonly experienced in group and in life. A common issue that comes up in consultation meetings is therapists being reluctant to present to their patient what they have identified as the patient's contributions to their problems. They are concerned about inducing guilt and shame in the patient. They fear "retraumatizing" the patient. They are unsettled by the possibility that it was going to be experienced by the patient as "blaming the victim."

My experience has shown that there is indeed a delicate line between the question, "What is your nickel in the dime?" and a patient's feeling that you are blaming the victim. One of the benefits of group is to have the opportunity to witness, *in vivo*, how the patient relates in the world of interpersonal challenges (Ormont, 1992). Eventually, every patient will "pepper the air" with parts of themselves and evoke reactions in other group members that will parallel what they evoke in others in their lives.

It is generally quite uncomfortable for patients to own that perhaps they have unintentionally contributed to problems they are having in the group that mirror the problems that brought them into therapy in the first place. Depending on the strength of the therapeutic alliance, as well as the ego strength of the patient, it will be more or less difficult for the patient to face how they are contributing to the problems they are complaining about in their lives.

Part of the therapeutic leverage of the group experience is that it provides an environment where it may be a bit less threatening to the patient when presented with and addressing their "nickel in the dime." Sometimes it is easier to hear this feedback from fellow groupmates than from the therapist.

When it occurs, it is not uncommon that patients will feel considerable shame, guilt, and/or embarrassment as a consequence of hearing the group's non-complementary feedback. At these times, when shame can be experienced as overwhelming, and becomes a barrier to a patient's learning, I try to soften the impact by using language that induces a gentler, milder experience. I use the frame of *upset* quite often when patients are experiencing great shame, guilt, self-hate, etc. Framing these overwhelming experiences as upset seems to soften their impact.

> "I can see how upset you are in acknowledging your part in this problem."

> "Can you explore what's inside your upset?"

> "Can you explore what's below the shame?"

I will then try to have others in the group join this patient in having engaged in behaviors that they are ashamed and embarrassed of.

> "Who can join Ruth in experiencing how hard it is to admit to yourself that you also may have inadvertently hurt someone through your well-intentioned but misguided efforts?"

The Parable of the Sixteenth Dragon

I may at times recount what I once heard as *The Parable of the Sixteenth Dragon*.

> The confident young knight was told that, in order to become a member of King Arthur's round table, he had to demonstrate his worth by slaying 16 dragons in 16 days. Accepting the challenge, while at the same time feeling intimidated by the prospect of slaying one dragon, much less 16, he gathered up his courage and departed for the land of the dragons.
>
> For 15 days he was able to overcome each ferocious beast he faced. With each victory he became more arrogant, boastful, and full of himself. On the 16th day he encountered the 16th dragon. This dragon, which was no more powerful or intimidating than any of the previous dragons, would not succumb to the young knight's efforts.
>
> This dragon had the ability to mirror every move the knight attempted to make. In its own way, it seemed to be a parallel of the knight. After a considerable battle, where there was no victor, the dragon spoke. "You have triumphed over the dragons, but can you triumph over yourself?"
>
> The young knight did not understand. He continued to battle, but every one of his efforts was met with equal force. He continually lost his will and energy to fight until he remembered the dragon's words. He slowly began to recognize that the way to defeat the dragon was to address his own shortcomings of arrogance, pretension, and conceit. He put down his sword, acknowledging his weaknesses. The dragon vanished.

Upon returning to the palace, he was surprised to be greeted by King Arthur himself. The wise king looked at the young knight and said, "I am delighted to have you sit at the round table. You have come to understand that the most difficult victory is over oneself."

I recount this parable when patients struggle to understand "What is your nickel in the dime?"

Conflict vs. Deficit

I was trained to understand that it was helpful to recognize and distinguish between *conflict* and *deficit* when attempting to understand and approach a patient's internal processes.

Conflict

Conflict generally centers on what is emotionally acceptable and tolerable to the patient and what is not. We can recognize conflict in the symptoms reflecting defensive patterns that patients use to ward off uncomfortable, unacceptable, and/or intolerable experiences. Common examples that we see in group are:

Intellectualization
Dysfunctional roles
Avoidance of intolerable experience
Projection
Projective identification
Acting out of split-off emotion

Al was very active and popular in group. He reliably gave advice, supported his groupmates, and disclosed the alcohol addiction that led him to Alcoholics Anonymous. While he was very open about his difficulties in the past, he rarely showed vulnerability in his present experience. When opening up about his struggles with alcohol, he spoke of it as if the challenges that led to his drinking were things he had conquered a long time ago. He presented himself as an elder statesman in dealing with addiction and the emotional problems that led to his substance abuse.

At first, his groupmates appreciated his openness and support. Over time, several members became very irritated and frustrated with him. One member, Ruth, suggested that she experienced his posture of having solved all his problems long ago as being very elevated and distancing.

Ruth said, "Al acts as if he doesn't have any problems now. Wasn't he in group because of issues he had with his wife that threatened their marriage?" We explored his groupmates' irritation with him. Al suddenly became very upset and defensive.

He complained that he didn't feel appreciated. Didn't his opening up about his struggle with alcohol show vulnerability? He angrily protested, "I don't know what you want!" He was indignant. He felt unappreciated. He wanted to quit.

I asked Al if he could take a step back and be curious about the feedback he was hearing. I suggested that it seemed he was taking in the feedback personally. He took a breath and stayed quiet for a moment. I wasn't certain whether he had cooled down enough to just be curious about what was being said to him.

I asked him what he was experiencing in his silence. In a low tone, Al admitted that his groupmates' complaints about him sounded familiar. They echoed his wife's complaints during their heated fights. She would accuse him of being "arrogant and elevated." He would tend to dismiss her complaints as "just busting my balls."

We gently explored how he tended to split off his own vulnerability and project it into someone else he was close with (his wife, his groupmates who were struggling). Seeing the vulnerability in someone he cared about would lead him to a "rescue fantasy," resulting in his taking on a rescuer role.

Eventually, he put two and two together and realized that this was his role in his loving but dysfunctional family. Al was always validated and praised for his "perspective and advice." It seems that both his strong-willed mother and his rather passive father had a tendency to parentify Al.

Al's mother and father would frequently become overwhelmed by family issues that would lead to their solution of attacking each other. He found that he could calm the family's anxiety by volunteering a solution. The content of his solutions was not as important as the process of stabilizing his parents' anxiety. He took on the role of the calming voice in the family.

In his rescuer role, he made sure his voice was strong, his eyes were focused on you, and he would speak in an authoritative tone, even though he might have had no idea what he was talking about. This rescuer role served him well in the context of the challenges he faced in his family of origin. It didn't work as well in the current context of the group and, more importantly, in his marriage.

Al found this exploration to be extremely helpful. He had a very good sense of humor, and when his group members "forbade" him to give advice or support in group he went along with it. He was encouraged to explore what came up in him when he had the impulse to help.

As a result of his group work, he reported noticing when he would go into his rescuer role with his wife. He learned to become curious about what activated this role and discovered that it was his discomfort with his wife's vulnerability. He was afraid of losing her. He worked on recognizing his own anxiety in seeing his wife struggle with issues that overwhelmed her. He became more aware of his impulse to contain his anxiety by elevating himself and speaking down to her while giving her unsolicited advice. Over time, Al reported that his relationship with his wife, while still having problems, had improved dramatically.

Deficit

A patient's deficits can be considered to be a function of their never having had experiences and role models to teach them essential processes such as self-regulation, frustration tolerance, effective interpersonal language, etc.

An example of a deficit appeared when Al was able to recognize and identify a desire to participate in group but didn't know what he wanted to say. He knew how to be a helper. However, he was "forbidden" by the group to help. Helping was second nature to him. Now he found himself very unsure of how to relate in group.

Al, who had been one of the more active members in group, said very little over the next few sessions. When asked what was going on, he replied that he knew how to help others, had the urge to help others, but did not have words other than the words of being a helper. He wanted to say something but did not know what to say.

He was very sincere in revealing his newly experienced awkwardness and discomfort in group. His groupmates suggested that that was a good start. He responded, "What was a good start?" His groupmates made it clear that he was finally showing his vulnerability by admitting that he didn't know what to say. *That* was the good start.

As a result of his tendency to tease, joke, and be increasingly open to feedback, his groupmates suggested a solution to his dilemma. When he had the impulse to say something but didn't have the words, he was to tell the group, and they would give him a multiple choice. The multiple choice would be a selection of feelings and experiences that they would have had if they were in his shoes.

He was very open to that solution. He began to ask for and utilize the multiple-choice possibilities, even if they didn't feel exactly right. Over time, he reported how his expanding emotional vocabulary affected him in ways he did not expect. He realized he was less anxious in group.

He didn't realize how anxious he would become when he didn't have the helper role to rely on. He realized that this underlying anxiety was regularly felt by him in group and at home. What use was he to anyone when he wasn't helping?

Al reported feeling more connected to his groupmates. More importantly, he reported how his therapy was changing the emotional tone at home with his wife. We experienced the difference in him as well.

Flooding

When a patient presents with a barrage of explanations, tangential points, or *non sequiturs*, I may suggest to them that they may be *flooding* us as well as themselves. This generally piques their interest. Sometimes they feel criticized. They may feel embarrassed. They may not understand what I mean.

I usually tell them that I'm sure that they are doing their best to communicate their experience. However, it seems they are experiencing something internally that is producing a pressure behind their communication, which is making it hard for others to understand and digest what they are saying.

This normally leads me to ask for the patient's experience behind the communication. They frequently respond that they are feeling flooded with emotion. We then can explore inside the flood.

> "Can you slow down the words and explore what's inside the flood that's coming up inside of you?"

This exploration can evolve into a mutual assumption, presuming that when they are speaking in a pressured manner they are likely splitting off the awareness of strong emotion. This emotion is now evident in the communication pattern that we are identifying as flooding.

Addressing Breakdowns in Communication

I have found that using the right word at the right time can help open up a patient's perspective to what was unknown to them. When this occurs, there can be an experience that is very rewarding for the patient and therapist. At times, however, I have also found myself making an observation or using a word that induces a very strong negative reaction in the patient. Sometimes this feedback is very difficult for a patient to hear; I may be on the wrong track.

I am usually surprised by the reaction because I clearly wasn't empathically attuned to the patient at that moment. In these instances, I attempt to take a breath and stay curious. Staying curious about their reaction helps me stay centered. I try to regress in the service of the patient's ego. I attempt to stay alert to being empathically attuned. What this requires is for me to imagine what it is like for this particular patient to be in their shoes, not what it would be like for me to be in their shoes.

I keep in mind what Agazarian (1997) describes as "systems in survival." Systems that are in survival are shaky and need to keep out differences. However, systems need differences to develop and transform. A solution to this dilemma is to introduce a difference that is not too different.

Frequently, I find that a particular word or thought has a connotation or association for the patient that is very different from what I had intended to communicate. In any case, I didn't recognize how vulnerable the patient was at that moment and took the strength of our therapeutic alliance for granted.

This situation generally happens when language I use connotes intolerable thoughts leading to intolerable feelings. Words such as *hate, dependency,* and *remorse* frequently evoke strong and sometimes unexpected reactions.

"How can you say that I hate my son, mother, etc.?"

"I don't depend on you or anyone."

"Why should I feel guilt, shame, remorse?"

My goal is to reassure my patients that their experience, no matter what my intent, is far more important than the words I am using. I explore what their reaction is to what I am saying. Maintaining and reinforcing the therapeutic alliance with the patient is always more important than whatever I am trying to get across in the moment.

The Defensive Use of Asking Questions

Patients ask questions of one another all the time. Occasionally, there will be a patient whose questions are incessant, diverting, unrelated to what is being focused on. I have often found this to be a clue in recognizing that the questioner may be using the questions as a defense against their own vulnerable experience.

I explore for the energy/impulse motivating their questions and encourage them to become curious. I generally ask:

"What's your feeling below your question?"

"What was your experience just before you started asking the questions?"

Not infrequently the response is, "I don't know." I will then ask,

"If you did know, what would your experience be?"

I ask them to slow down and reflect for a moment. Usually, they will recognize they were having strong emotions that they wanted to move away from by moving to their head and asking the questions. If they still can't find their experience, I might ask the group what their experience is like when Riley is asking all these questions. I frame it this way to bring their attention to the here and now.

Chapter 14

The Use of Fables

Therapy is serious business, but that does not mean we cannot be playful as we approach our work. I have used fables lightheartedly to reinforce perspectives that are sometimes difficult for the patient to swallow. I make use of certain fables that are well known, taking themes from them for my purposes and then changing them a bit for brevity.

Kissing the Frog

The fable of the prince who was turned into a frog by a sorcerer's spell goes a long way in helping patients find a way to break the deadlock with someone they are angry at, furious with, not trusting of, etc. This story can be surprisingly useful in breaking out of an intransigent role lock. I might tell a group member my version of the fable:

> "Do you remember the fable of the witch whose spell turned the prince into a frog? The only way to break the spell would be for someone who is worthy to kiss the frog, who then would be restored to his natural princely form and then be available to you."

Generally, patients do not like hearing this, since it implies that in order to break the spell (role lock) they have to kiss the person they are upset with, have disdain for, hate, etc. Kissing the frog entails helping the patient recognize similarities with the offending individual and becoming empathically attuned to the person they cannot stand. It can also help the patient recognize split off parts of themselves that they are projecting into the member they cannot tolerate.

If they can find their way to kissing the frog, it often has surprisingly positive results. I tend to tease my patients a bit when they respond, "Why do I have to kiss the frog?" I smile and say, "You don't have to. However, if you choose to follow this thinking, it may be the key to finding a way out of the bind you're in with this person. If you have a better way, let me know."

DOI: 10.4324/9781003649632-14

The Three Little Pigs

I use the fable of the Three Little Pigs when patients are struggling with frustration tolerance.

> Do you remember the story of the three little pigs? The first little pig quickly built a flimsy house of straw and laughed at his brother pigs, who continued to work on their houses, which was taking more effort. The second little pig built his house out of twigs, which took a while longer, but was not much stronger than the first little pig's house of straw.
>
> They both laughed disparagingly at the third little pig, who was putting in more time, care, and labor in building a sturdy house of bricks. They taunted and judged the third little pig for working so hard and long. They had their houses, and their houses were built with much less effort.
>
> In their haste, they denied how flimsy their houses were. They ignored how vulnerable they were to the problem that they faced in the first place—the Big Bad Wolf. Of course, the whole point of building their houses was to protect them from the Big Bad Wolf, if and when he finally appeared. Their houses were fine as long as the wolf wasn't around.

Of course, we know the end of this story. Only the third little pig's house could withstand the ominous wolf when he threatened, "I'll huff, and I'll puff, and I'll blow your house down."

Sooner or later, the wolves in our lives appear. Are we looking for immediate gratification that might give us rapid results but may not be enough to insulate us from the inevitable wolf? Or are we going to remember the third little pig who, even though it took more effort, built a solid house that was resilient against the inevitable challenges that we all will, at some point, have to face.

I use this fable often when patients ask me "How long is this therapy going to take? I heard different types of therapy only take six months." I answer with this fable. I tell them that I try to follow the lesson of the third little pig. Then I ask, "Which little pig are you?"

Sleeping Beauty

I have used the fable of Sleeping Beauty when a patient has a great deal of trouble initiating activity in group but when approached seems to come alive very quickly. I inquire if they remember the fable of Sleeping Beauty. Most members only remember the part of her waking up when she was kissed by the prince. I occasionally tease the person that they seem to have qualities similar to Sleeping Beauty. This usually gets the member's and the group's attention.

I ask, "Who put the spell on you that made you so quiet when you clearly have so much to say?" I then try to spread this exploration past this particular member into an exploration of other members' experiences of holding back in group. I might explore, "Who put you to sleep?" and what their experience is like when they are "kissed" (approached) in the group.

Icarus

I have used the Greek myth of Icarus when working with patients who would get themselves into a bind because of their arrogance and hubris. I recount the story of Icarus, the son of a master craftsman who constructs wings made of feathers and wax in order to escape their imprisonment. Icarus was instructed to fly neither too low (out of complacency) nor too high (as a result of hubris). In his excitement, Icarus flies too high and gets too close to the sun. His wings of wax melt, and he falls into the sea.

I find this myth works well with patients who present with grandiosity, ultimately finding themselves isolated in the group. This often is a surprise to the group member, who generally does not realize how they are turning off relationships in group as well as in their outside lives. "I guess I was feeling too full of myself" is a common response when the patient recognizes how they are elevating themselves above their groupmates.

Ben was well-intentioned but quite clueless about how being "helpful and instructive" could be experienced as arrogant and elevated. He appreciated learning about how he could unwittingly antagonize others. He realized that this might have contributed to problems he had with his partner. I would tease Ben, calling him Icarus when this side of him would emerge in group. He would generally respond with a big sheepish and grateful smile.

The (Other) Parable of the Sixteenth Dragon

There is another version of the sixteenth dragon parable that I have found to be useful in helping patients understand the concept of the transitional object.

The eager young knight was told that in order to become a member of King Arthur's round table he had to demonstrate his worth by slaying 16 dragons in 16 days. After accepting the challenge, while at the same time feeling intimidated by the prospect of slaying one dragon, much less 16, he wandered the halls of the castle and happened to run into Merlin, the magician. "What troubles you?" Merlin asked the young knight. The knight responded that he had to slay 16 dragons in 16 days if he was to become a member of King Arthur's court. He wasn't sure if he was up to the task. Merlin smiled and told the knight to follow him. Merlin stopped and peeked into a closet. He then proceeded to look for and found a sword that he graciously gave to the young fellow. Merlin wished the knight good fortune with the dragons and went on his way.

The young knight was delighted. He told himself that with Merlin's sword he now had the power to confront the dragons. He gathered his courage and departed for the land of the dragons. Day after day, the young knight succeeded in slaying his quota of dragons, 16 dragons in 16 days. Having completed his test, he returned home and was welcomed warmly and praised for his substantial accomplishment.

The next day, the young knight ran into Merlin. Merlin congratulated him on achieving such a challenging test of skill. Excitedly, the knight thanked Merlin, saying his success was solely due to his having Merlin's magic sword as his weapon. Merlin, looking confused, responded, "What magic sword? That sword was some old relic I took out of my utility closet."

I have found this story to be an effective way of presenting the concept of the *transitional object*. I suggest that group can be considered a reliable transitional object in our effort to move into the world.

Chapter 15

Challenging Moments in Group

Addressing Potentially Explosive Topics

An important headline of the day often makes its way into group. The political environment affects all of us, and inevitably group members will bring up topics that are important to them. These topics are typically emotionally charged. I have found that successfully facilitating these potentially volatile moments generally requires me to help differentiate the group member's emotional process from the content of the issue.

MAL: "I want to talk about D.E.I."

PAT: "What's D.E.I.?"

MAL: "Diversity, equity, and inclusion. Where have you been?"

EVA: "Yes, these programs are being threatened."

PAT: "I thought we weren't supposed to talk about topics in group."

MAL: "This is more than a topic. It's dealing with the issues that have held people like me back in this society."

ERIN: "I know that it's an important topic, but Arthur keeps stopping us from talking about topics."

ARTHUR: "Yes, it's an important topic but, as Erin reminds us, we don't talk about topics in group. That doesn't stop us from exploring our experiences related to the content of the topic that may be right below the surface of our desire to engage in a discussion or debate."

I was instructed early in my training to point out to group members that when topics such as religion or politics come up we don't talk about topics in the group. Actually, we don't talk about anything in the group. Our goal is to explore our feelings and experiences that are aroused and activated in us in relationship to the topics that may come up.

ARTHUR: "So, Mal, could you take a moment and explore your experience regarding how D.E.I. has affected you?"

MAL: "What do you mean?"

DOI: 10.4324/9781003649632-15

ARTHUR: "What are you feeling below your desire to talk about D.E.I.? Take a moment and reflect on what your experience is below your words."

MAL: "I'm upset. I'm scared."

ARTHUR: "Can you look inside your fear and tell us what you see?"

MAL: "I don't know what I see."

ARTHUR: "Can anyone resonate with Mal and look inside their experience related to what Mal may be experiencing?"

ARIK: "If I were sitting in Mal's seat, I'd be fearing losing what D.E.I. has accomplished for me out in the world. I feel it too."

This short example demonstrates how I immediately attempt to shift the focus of the exploration in group from the topic (content) to the underlying experience of the group member or members who are bringing it up (process). I intervene quickly because these topics often contain volatile emotions connected to the content of the issue.

In one very cohesive group, when members casually revealed or implied who they voted for in a recent election (content), one member remained silent (process). In exploring his silence, we discovered that he was reluctant to admit who he voted for. He did not trust that his groupmates would understand the motivations for his choice and would reject him.

DAN: "Why is Dario so quiet? What's going on, Dario?"

DARIO: "What do you mean?"

SUE: "Come on, Dario. You started looking down when people started sharing their experience of the election."

DARIO: "You're right. I don't trust you to accept my choice."

ARTHUR: "Dario, could you take a moment and reflect on your experience below your negative prediction?"

DARIO: "I feel great anxiety."

ARTHUR: "Take a moment and look inside your anxiety."

DARIO: "I'm afraid that I'll lose the closeness of my groupmates."

CARL: "I can't believe you voted for X."

ARTHUR: "Carl, what is your experience below your words?"

CARL: "I feel scared. This reminds me of my family where, as you know, I couldn't trust anyone."

The continued exploration of group members' experiences below their thoughts (content), judgments, and opinions opened up to experiences of trusting and losing intimate relationships, keeping secrets, and fears of being cast out (process).

Group members often ask me to give them room to talk about issues that are weighing on them. They know my tendency is to immediately remind them that, "We don't do topics in our therapy group. Our focus is on how the content of the topic is affecting us."

Every once in a while, I am tempted to let the group talk about the issues that are weighing on them without directing them to the underlying process. It inevitably devolves into the kind of debates and arguments members experience in their outside lives. I eventually ask them to explore their experience below the argument, debate, or silence. That is where we find meaning.

Useful Interventions in Challenging Moments

"So, what is your experience like when I'm unfair, speaking too much, saying too little, heavy-handed, etc.?"

"What is the group avoiding by being silent, fighting with each other, or me?"

"Should I soft-pedal what I see?"

"What problem is the group solving by scapegoating Jill?"

"What problem is Jack solving by letting himself be scapegoated?"

"Who else gets irritated [self-hating, despairing, disappointed] when they do the same thing over and over again?"

I have found these types of inquiries to be very useful in helping members during difficult group moments to shift to an observer perspective and stop the group from creating, or someone volunteering to become, an identified patient. It can help create an atmosphere of safety and curiosity. Yvonne Agazarian was very helpful in introducing me to this manner of group-as-a-whole thinking.

Dealing With the Elephant in The Room

The "elephant in the room" is a classic phrase describing an environment of avoidance, where group members are aware that there are potentially explosive issues that are being assiduously avoided and not addressed in the group process (Ormont, 1992). I have witnessed and experienced this type of group environment being a grave threat to the group's cohesiveness and therapeutic potential if not handled well.

I have had many patients report former group experiences where they were terrified of revealing themselves for fear of "blowing up the group" or "being horribly attacked." Inevitably, they left their former group without revealing their experience. These patients were among the most reluctant to give group therapy another chance. As a result of this potential explosiveness, the group environment can be an overwhelming challenge for the therapist who does not have a framework for how to approach this delicate process, and has not experienced working through this type of volatile situation.

Even with years of experience, this highly charged group environment can provoke strong transference and countertransference reactions. I have experienced groups where members would remain silent while communicating through deliberately provocative nonverbal behavior. This can take the form of arriving late, avoiding eye contact, heavy breathing, and deliberately looking out the window in a passive-aggressive manner.

One approach that I found doesn't work well is asking members who were part of a polarized moment what they are feeling. It can be, and frequently is, an exploration that moves into blaming and complaining about the other members. I approach this potentially explosive group environment by continuously highlighting the norms and goals of the group as well as the individual goals of the group members.

The process I have adopted is:

1   I do not ask for a patient's feelings but inquire about a member's experiences. When members respond with blaming and complaining, I ask them to explore for the experience below their heated words.
2   At this point, I frequently bring up the norms in the group. I attempt to shift group members' focus from their heart to their head.
3   I remind the group that our goal is to stay connected to ourselves internally while at the same time staying connected interpersonally. This ability requires that we not take feedback and other members' reactions personally.
4   I ask group members to keep in mind their "nickel in the dime." How are they contributing to the group situation that they are involved in?
5   I point out that the group experience requires us to adopt two contrasting perspectives, alternating back and forth between the two: the observing self and the experiential self. I go through this process in order to lessen the heat in the room. I am deliberately attempting to move the group from an emotional to a more cerebral experience. When it is very hot, members frequently challenge my attempt at cooling things down. I remind them that one of our primary goals in group is to be effective.

"My goal is fuck you, is that effective enough?" a patient once responded to this intervention. I answered by asking the group if there were others in the group whose goal was "fuck you." My attempt at being non-defensive in the face of this provocation (which weighed against my silent desire to respond with a wholesome "fuck you, as well") fortunately resulted in breaking some of the tension in the group.

I was trying to model for the group how not to take feedback personally. This time it worked. If we are fortunate, this type of tension-filled group episode will last a relatively short time and be unpacked within a few sessions.

In contrast, I have experienced a group "frozen" in avoidance that lasted several months. Members would address many issues while avoiding the underlying tension that was experienced by everyone. The source of the tension centered on two members of the group. After reinforcing our group norms, I would, as usual, gently explore our group members' present experiences in the here and now.

Usually, someone inevitably exposes how uncomfortable they are feeling and how they are avoiding addressing certain issues. I follow that up by exploring if other group members are avoiding something and what their experience is like in their avoidance. These explorations may last a short period or for many sessions. Either way, my approach is the same.

In the case of the "frozen" group, I kept my eye on the two members who were holding what appeared to be explosive anger. I looked for any change in their physical posture and facial changes.

When I noticed any change, which sometimes did not shift for months, I gently suggested, "I noticed a little change in you. Am I correct?" More often than not the patient responded with some sort of opening such as, "I'm hesitant to say this, but ... ." Simply having them say anything, generally, lowered the "heat" in the room.

Once the emotional temperature in the room cools down, I can explore members' experiences of what is happening (now) in the group (not what *happened*, which generally leads to a dead end of intellectualizing and explaining). I find it grounding to remember what group members are specifically working on in their therapy.

I attempt to bring into the group experience explorations as to how members may be responding to a tense situation in their characteristic roles (e.g., victim, passive, quiet observer, rescuer). I point out that this is a great opportunity to engage a potentially volatile situation in a different manner. This process is not easy and often does not neatly unfold in the manner I just outlined.

When I have been successful, I believe my being able to remain separate and "stay larger than the moment" has contributed to the outcome. What generally happens is that the members holding the antagonistic split in the group eventually begin to open up and relate through their experience of what they were going through and what they are experiencing now.

Other group members explore their experiences as well. The general sense in the group is great relief. Going through this type of experience, which is ultimately resolved, is reported to be very meaningful for members of the group. I have to admit it has been very rewarding for me as well.

I was once told that because of my "swag" (my supposedly self-assured guidance through the experience), my appearing to be not intimidated by the situation calmed things down and lent itself to a successful outcome. At the time, I did not know that "swag" meant swagger. I appreciated the validation. It did not correspond to my internal experience of tension while facilitating the group.

It has been my experience that these enactments, if successfully worked through, frequently end up with members feeling less intimidated and more prepared to deal with polarized moments in the group. These group experiences, if successful, can contribute to the group's cohesiveness. If not successful, they can undermine a group's functioning.

A sign of cohesion is evident to me when patients can laugh at themselves while recounting how they behaved when they were "in fight." One member recently recalled how he acted out aggressively toward another groupmate, saying, "I can't believe I picked up that chair and was going to throw it." This actually happened when I still had my office.

A successful resolution to this type of potentially explosive group experience can contribute to group members taking more chances in group. It reassures members that they will not be killed or kill off the group if they bring in something that really upsets other members. Patients have described this type of experience and the resolution of it as one of their most meaningful group learnings.

Witnessing Repair in Group

As I just recounted, attempting to unpack the emotions that the elephant in the room may be containing is a very delicate undertaking that requires steadiness and patience. I have consulted with many therapists who reported avoiding dealing with their elephant in the room. This avoidance would tend to contribute to the group becoming polite, unsafe, boring, and essentially "dead in the water."

The process I described in the previous section has been very helpful in keeping me insulated from being provoked by the very powerful emotions that the group is avoiding and can emerge at any time. A positive outcome that stands out for many patients having gone through a highly charged and polarized group process is the witnessing of a successful repair. The more extreme the breakdown, the more group members report feeling "freed up" by the experience of a repair.

Many patients report never having witnessed this in their families or having experienced it in their current lives. In exploring their experience of the repair, members frequently comment on how meaningful it was, and what a great relief it was to see two or more people truly mending a breach that seemed impossible to resolve.

The Experience of Remorse

I find it helpful in these situations to keep in mind Klein's description of what she called the *depressive position* (Kibel, 1993). I describe this idea to the group when the patient is finally able to see that the bad (withholding) group member is the same person as the supportive good (loving, providing) group member. In recognizing that they are one and the same person, group members who were polarized often experience *remorse*.

The experience of remorse can be understood to be the outcome of integrating the good and bad split. We can now experience ourselves (me) and the object (not me) in terms of Winnicott's (1971) concept of being "good enough."

How Not to Repair

Explaining instead of apologizing: "I didn't mean to hurt you; I was only trying to … ." I have frequently witnessed patients attempting to repair a breach with another groupmate and digging themselves deeper into a hole. One pattern that frequently fails is when a group member explains what they intended, or what they thought, rather than simply apologizing by showing regret and remorse. "I was only trying to …" generally is not received well as a repair. It tends to fog over a direct admission of regret or remorse. "I'm sorry that you feel this way" usually does not work very well either.

I have had quite a few patients over the years comment on how hurt and upset they have been when their attempts at repair were rejected or not appreciated. Repair generally requires an acknowledgment that I did do something that adversely affected you. The group experience can help members recognize how they may have been echoing the failed attempts at repair that they witnessed in their families.

In exploring what prevented them from simply apologizing or expressing remorse, many patients would identify an underlying emotional barrier related to not being able to tolerate the shame or guilt related to adversely affecting someone else and being "wrong." This exploration can lead to very meaningful work related to tolerating guilt and shame.

Tolerating Guilt and Shame

Frequently shame and embarrassment will emerge in moments of potential learning. As I covered earlier in the section addressing a patient's "nickel in the dime," the therapist has the delicate challenge of pointing out how the patient has actually contributed to their problems in the group and in their lives (Ormont, 1992).

I try to soften the impact of this emotional learning by using language that conveys a softer, milder experience, as shame can be experienced as overwhelming and become a barrier to a patient's learning. I frequently reflect back to a patient that she seems upset when she says that she cannot tolerate the shame of what she did. I use the term *upset* quite often when patients are experiencing great shame, guilt, self-hate, etc. Framing these overwhelming experiences as upset seems to soften their impact.

"I can see how upset you are in acknowledging your part in this problem."

I will then attempt to have others in the group join this patient in exploring how difficult it is to cope with the feelings of shame and guilt when acknowledging their contribution to an interpersonal problem.

Recognizing Cognitive Dissonance in Group

Festinger's (1957) theory of *cognitive dissonance* has been very helpful to me in understanding challenging moments that frequently come up in group. The group moment described below is characterized by a situation where a patient cannot see or hear (or will not permit themselves to see or hear) a salient part of what is transpiring, leading them to react to a very distorted impression of what is happening.

> Mary became very upset and angry at Sam for having "blown off" the first meeting after our summer break. Mary was very invested in Sam and was a great support over the years in his struggle to "show up" in uncomfortable situations. When Sam was asked why he did not attend, he responded that he mistakenly made a dentist appointment that over-lapped with the group meeting and decided that he did not want to go through the trouble of rearranging it.
>
> It was upon hearing this that Mary became upset, and said angrily, "I'm done with Sam. After all this time he still won't extend himself for anyone." One of Mary's issues was her tendency to go into a helper role that would ultimately result in disappointment. Upon hearing Mary, Sam went into his role of pseudo-self-sufficient victim and responded with his usual, "See? It always ends up this way, I don't need this."
>
> I asked Mary to explore below her upset and see what was there. After a moment, she said, "Sam is kind, smart, and can be empathically attuned. However, after all this time, and all we've done for him, when I see him not making any effort at all on our behalf, I feel completely taken for granted. I'm done." I asked Sam what his reaction was to Mary's comment. His indignant response was, "*She's* done? *I'm* done."
>
> I asked the group if anyone could join either Sam or Mary. Beth, who had been working on her tendency when upset to split the world into good and bad, pointed out that Mary had said some very supportive things and Sam only responded to "I'm done." Beth volunteered that she had a tendency to do the same thing. "When I'm in my victim role, I only see and hear the bad in what the other person said or did. I don't hear the whole communication. Sam didn't hold onto Mary's acknowledging his positive qualities [kind, smart]." At that point Sam cooled down and said, "I didn't hear any of that. I only heard Mary say, 'I'm done'."

This is an example of the common situation of having group members witness how someone under stress selectively hears, sees, and takes in what is familiar to them, editing out data that doesn't conform to what they have experienced in their lives. This selective editing of reality that does not conform to what is consistent with their established beliefs can lead patients to frame their experience in a way that reinforces the self-fulfilling prophecy of a dysfunctional role.

Under stress, patients frequently have distorted perceptions of reality that are the result of what is known as *cognitive dissonance*. Cognitive dissonance leads a person to reduce the stress of having to experience reality that is inconsistent with what they believe. They reduce this stress by avoiding contradictory data or information. They tend to rationalize away what is not consistent with their expectations, based on their belief system.

I believe this was illustrated by Sam's experience. Sam only heard Mary say, "I'm done." He did not take in Mary's mentioning his positive qualities. This was an example of Sam's being in a victim role. His expectation was that people inevitably would betray and leave him. He did not hear Mary's validating remarks about him that might have tempered his self-protective response.

The group process provides the opportunity to witness and experience, *in vivo*, how the patient distorts what is being said in a way that frequently does not emerge in individual treatment. This is a good example of the value of not believing or disbelieving what patients report in their treatment. Generally, in my experience, when this sort of distortion appears in the group, patients frequently do not at first believe what is being said about how they misread a situation.

Dealing with Cognitive Dissonance

When dealing with patients who are not open to the feedback that their perception may be distorted, I would ask, "What would your experience be like if you could accept that you were editing out an important aspect of the interaction, and that distorts your perception of what occurred?"

Patients who have difficulty accepting that they may be distorting their experience frequently respond with the following pattern:

1 *Denial*, reinforced by explanations and rationalizations.
2 *Confusion* at first, leading to an uncomfortable acceptance. Taking in the feedback of group members they trust can thin out the resistance to accepting that perhaps their perceptions were distorted.
3 *Shame* related to not recognizing what they were doing in group. Feeling very vulnerable and exposed.
4 *Guilt* connected to the realization that they may be engaging in this same pattern with important dependency relationships outside of the group.
5 *Remorse* that they may have hurt those they accused of hurting them.
6 *Relief* in understanding how they may be contributing to some of the issues they are complaining about in therapy. They finally recognize their

"nickel in the dime." Frequently patients will report that they never really understood this phrase or how it applied to them.

In my experience, this is a very delicate process. It is generally easy to witness someone else distorting what is going on in their experience. It is not that easy to acknowledge that you, yourself, have been distorting and contributing to a situation that you indignantly felt a victim of. It can be difficult to admit to yourself that you may have been a major contributor to your own problems.

The Good Fortune of Being in a Group with Members You Can't Stand

Patients frequently complain about fellow group members. Complaints generally center on intense negative reactions that the complaining patient is experiencing in relationship to a particular groupmate. Sometimes they ask to switch groups, knowing that I have several to choose from.

After exploring their complaint, I suggest that the group member who stirs up such intense negative feelings is generally the most important person in the group for them. I ask them to bring these feelings into the group. I present the idea that the individuals who provoke strong judgmental feelings frequently parallel experiences with problematic intimate relationships in our lives (Ormont, 1992; Yalom & Leszcz, 2005).

Patients generally push back and say they wouldn't associate with this type of person in their outside lives. I suggest that the characteristics that they are complaining about in certain groupmates may reflect intolerable parts of themselves or parts of others who they love or must be in a relationship with (such as a spouse or a boss).

I suggest that being able to recognize and work through their strong negative reactions to these particular members can aid in not being hijacked by their own reactions that may be inadvertently contributing to undermining important love and work relationships. Patients frequently are first surprised then reluctantly accept that there may be some therapeutic value in working on relationships with members they do not like or respect. Some patients are intrigued by this prospect. Some just give me the benefit of the doubt.

More often than not, something occurs in the group that centers on the particular person some member may have been complaining about. It frequently leads to an enactment in the group. Complaints such as, "I can't stand his passiveness," "She talks in circles," "He's so judgmental," are an opportunity to explore why the patient has such an intense reaction to those qualities in others. I ask, "Why does it bother you so much?" I take into consideration that extreme reactions are frequently a sign that the patient is going into a dysfunctional role.

At this point, I try to keep in mind the presenting complaint of the patient. It generally centers on interpersonal difficulties in intimacy leading to a vast array of resulting symptoms. These symptoms frequently present as isolation, unhappiness in intimate relationships, depression, generalized anxiety, etc.

It is often the case that when we explore and expand on what their experience is, patients report recognizing that a similar pattern occurs with significant others or work relationships. Very often, the qualities that they cannot stand in a group member will be recognized as being a split off quality the patient has within themselves. The extreme reactions provoked by other group members have been a very useful window into exploring the projections, projective identifications, roles, and role locks that contribute to the issues that patients bring into their therapy.

The Experience of Safety in Group

Safety in group is of primary importance. We cannot undertake useful therapeutic work without both patients and ourselves feeling safe. Over the years, I have found that *safety* means different things to different patients. Some patients report feeling safe when they feel comfortable; others feel safe when they are in a familiar environment. Some patients use the formidable word *unsafe* when they feel moderately uncomfortable. Others do not use that term until they feel an overwhelming experience of threat. Sometimes demanding safety can be used as a means of controlling others.

I believe that the foundation for a sense of safety in group rests on an experience where the patient feels sure that the environment they are in is in the interest of their growth and development, even if it means, at times, feeling uncomfortable or very upset.

This experience includes being challenged and challenging, being comfortable and uncomfortable, and not taking feedback personally. The goal is to develop a sense of increased self-esteem and mastery that results from facing (and possibly resolving) difficult challenges in group. Safety is the outcome of this experience.

In my groups, establishing the norms of knowing only each member's first name and not having contact outside of the group meetings are the first concrete steps in developing a context that can be very reassuring to members. Members frequently report that these norms add to their feeling of safety.

Since safety has different connotations for different patients, I make it a point to explore fully any comments that allude to their feeling safe or feeling unsafe. These explorations have revealed a wide range of different experiences and attitudes in relation to what it means to feel safe.

I am always attempting to establish a sense of safety with my patients while at the same time helping them develop the ability to tolerate the feelings that emerge from being in the group experience. These feelings can range from feeling very pleasant, warm, and open to feeling extremely uncomfortable, emotionally exposed, and overwhelmed.

Moments in the group can often be experienced as unsafe. Some patients say they do not feel safe when someone challenges them. Others report feeling unsafe because of the makeup of the group. Still others report feeling unsafe revealing anything personal about themselves.

Accepting at face value and not exploring and working through the protest that patients do not feel safe can throw a lot of "cold water" onto the group process. Patients start to tiptoe around each other. Group members tend to be more cautious in saying everything in order not to destabilize the member or members who feel unsafe.

I try to reinforce the notion that we are not here to pursue a safe space that requires that we avoid discomfort, difficult moments, and challenging experiences. We develop safety in group by being able to learn how to face up to and effectively deal with differences that can lead to difficult, challenging, and uncomfortable experiences.

Safety results from being able to find solutions to difficult moments. As reviewed in previous sections, learning how to deal with difficult internal and interpersonal feelings and experiences and witnessing the repair when breakdowns occur can increase members' sense of safety in the group.

In my experience, *safety emerges in a group as a side effect* of the group's ability to stay curious, not take feedback personally, and adopt the perspectives of the observing and experiential self. I have consulted with therapists who present cases to me that focus on their having difficulty when a patient says they feel unsafe. They found themselves hesitant to explore what safety meant in the group, ironically, out of fear that the member who expressed feeling unsafe would again feel unsafe.

Some therapists report feeling intimidated when a patient accuses them of making them feel unsafe. Their solution was to apologize, back off, and not explore what that means. One practitioner recounted how she experienced a patient declaring that they felt unsafe to be a "stop sign" in exploration. The group process seemed to enter a period of avoidant politeness. Over time, the group seemed to be "dead in the water." The therapist felt bullied into obeying the unsafe stop sign. She began to experience concurrent countertransference in feeling unsafe herself.

My initial response with any issue related to safety is to explore the patient's experience in the same way we would explore any other experience. Some questions I might ask are:

"What's your experience like when you feel unsafe?"

"Can anyone else relate to feeling unsafe here in the group?"

"When and where did you experience this sense of unsafety before?"

As I mentioned earlier, I believe that a sense of safety should be an outgrowth of the experience of mastery generated by working through the challenges faced in group. I do not support developing a controlled environment that creates an artificial sense of safety for the patient by avoiding discomfort or challenging experiences. Patients frequently report that they felt increased safety when difficult issues and enactments that emerged in group were not avoided and, most importantly, were worked through in the group before their eyes.

Exploring the Experience of Safety

The experience of safety or unsafety frequently (though not always) reflects transference, or a patient going into a dysfunctional role in the group experience. The group experience presents patients with countless opportunities to react to look-alike events that occur in group. The look-alike events related to a patient's feeling safe or unsafe are ever-present.

> Alice, in group for three months, revealed angrily that she didn't feel safe in the group. I began to explore her experience of not feeling safe. She said that her groupmate Brad would pooh-pooh or explain away his behavior when she suggested that she was upset with him. "If I air a concern, he says something that wipes out my experience. He'll make a face, minimize what I'm saying, and the group won't say a word about it."
>
> In further exploring her experience of not feeling safe, she wondered why no one in the group said anything about her not feeling safe or joined her. She complained that others in the group regularly gave support to others but not to her.
>
> I asked her if she could stay curious and possibly reframe her complaint into a question. Angrily, she responded, "What do you mean, 'reframe my complaint'? Now I'm feeling wiped out by you. I'm not feeling safe with you."
>
> I asked her if she was curious about why it appeared that others in the group gave support to each other and not to her. I still was unable to elicit her curiosity or her observing self. Her response was to focus on my using the word *appear*. "What do you mean, it 'appeared'? It's really happening."
> I used this exchange to open it up to the group and asked, "Have others in the group noticed what Alice is saying? She sees everyone supporting everyone else but not giving support to her when she needs it."
>
> What emerged in the following group exploration was revealing. Group members shared that when Alice was upset about something that occurred in group she would frequently use language that seemed "sharp and accusing." Even her use of the word *unsafe* felt accusing. Several members revealed feeling cautious with her, ironically feeling unsafe with her.
>
> The ensuing exploration focused on the experience she felt below her experience of unsafety. She discovered that below *unsafe* were feelings of shame and a fear of retaliation, which recapitulated her experience of feeling unsafe during disagreements in her family of origin. Conversely, in

exploring her groupmates feeling unsafe with her, several suggested that they feared retaliation from her if they made her feel uncomfortable or unsafe.

Alice, whose presenting complaint focused on difficulties in intimate relationships and feelings of isolation, had difficulty hearing the feedback. At first, she became angry. I asked her to explore below the anger. She felt attacked. I asked her if she could try to take this feedback in as data and not take it personally. She admitted it was hard for her to believe that she could make others feel uncomfortable and intimidated.

She reported back next week that she noticed when she either thought or actually said that she felt unsafe several times that week while arguing with her husband. She remembered her group work, took a step back, and explored her feelings during the argument. She realized that below feeling unsafe, she felt "hurt and brokenhearted."

Instead of saying that she felt unsafe, which would have normally resulted in his retreating and ending the discussion, she revealed that "her feelings were hurt." Her husband, instead of retreating, stayed open to exploring how he was affecting her. She was surprised that such a little change in her communication could have such a significant effect on her husband. A part of her didn't trust that things could change that quickly. However, she was determined to keep an open mind.

She reported to the group that the previous week's group had a positive effect on how that typical fight was resolved. She described having a feeling of closeness to her husband that she hadn't felt in a long time. It was a concrete example of the parallel process which she never really understood before.

In exploring group members' experiences related to Alice's report, several expressed warmth, support, and relief. Some expressed hope that the group could actually survive very uncomfortable feelings. Several members said that going through this potentially explosive episode in group made them feel less unsafe in bringing up difficult issues with Alice and other group members that they generally avoided.

After this group experience, I noticed group members, more routinely, bringing up difficult or uncomfortable interpersonal group issues. I understood this to be a reflection of increased trust and group cohesion.

Chapter 16

Group Snapshots

A Solution to Being Lost in the Woods

On occasion, patients present with the complaint that they feel lost in their lives. I use this opportunity to ask if they know what some wilderness experts recommend when we find ourselves lost in the woods. I tell my patients that I am using a variation of those recommendations that could be useful in our work.

People who find themselves actually lost in the woods frequently will not admit to themselves that they are lost. Instead, they try to find their way by looking for landmarks or something familiar. Very often they find themselves deeper in the woods and still lost.

When patients express that they feel lost, I generally ask, "What do you imagine you should do first when you realize you're lost in the woods?" Common replies are, "Take out your compass, check out the location of the sun, retrace your steps, etc." I tell them *"No!"*

1. The first recommendation is to admit that you are lost.

   People are generally reluctant to admit that they are lost. Instead, they keep walking further into the woods, resulting in their being even more disoriented and still lost.

   I then ask, "What's next?" Usual replies are, "Take out your compass, look at the position of the sun, yell for help." I again say, *"No!"*

2. Second is *stop*. When you stop, you now have location. You may not know where your location is in relation to other locations but now at least you have a location.

   I then ask, "What's next?"

3. Mark your location (by building a small campfire, gathering some rocks, etc.).
4. Walk 50 paces in each direction—north, south, east, and west—coming back to your location after 50 paces.

DOI: 10.4324/9781003649632-16

5. Double the number of paces (going in all four directions).

6. Always come back to your location.

7. Keep repeating this pattern, always returning to your location, until you inevitably run into a stream, road, person, etc.

I believe an important step in your therapy is to admit to yourself that you're lost when you're lost. We can then follow the roadmap that I just outlined. We can consider our therapy sessions as your campfire and location. Our process is to focus on your issues, utilize our work in your life, and then bring these experiences back to our sessions to explore whether or not what we explored in session was helpful.

"This process represents the 50 paces of exploration, going back and forth from your location, which is now defined by our sessions. It's usually more productive than walking around in intellectual, emotionally split-off circles."

Reinforcing "What Do You Need from the Group Right Now?"

As I covered in an earlier section, patients will often bring up an issue that is unclear, not to the point, meandering, ambiguous, confusing, etc. I believe addressing this requires reinforcement throughout our work. Group members often respond to this member by asking a lot of questions, in an attempt to gain some clarity as to what he or she is trying to get across to the group. Sometimes other members become frustrated and irritated with the group member's struggle to be understood.

I generally ask the group what their experience is right below their questions. Generally, others in the group don't get what the patient who is speaking is looking for in the group. I find that my asking "What do you need from the group right now?" tends to surprise group members, who never really pay attention to why they are saying what they are saying.

Frequently, they are confused by my question. I respond again with, "Yes, remember our understanding is that all behavior has a purpose. I'm wondering what your purpose, what your goal is right now, in opening this up with the group." It is not unusual that the group member has no idea what they need from the group and has no idea what their goal is.

"I'm just opening up. Do I need a goal?" At this point I ask the group members what they think. "Do we need a goal when opening up in group?" often leads the group to an exploration that frequently surprises them and sometimes leaves them feeling uneasy. "I feel self-conscious when thinking of why I'm saying what I'm saying." My response is usually, "Is that a bad thing?"

Further exploration reveals that members often feel privately confused, timid, self-conscious, embarrassed, ashamed, etc. during conversations with others. However, they just let the moment pass, don't focus on it, and try to forget it. They just say what comes to their mind. Participating in group often calls attention to how self-conscious many group members feel in the interpersonal world.

Upon further exploration, members share how these experiences can contribute to self-doubt, withdrawal, generalized anxiety, or discomfort in interpersonal relationships, as well as low self-esteem and depression. I would then ask the group to explore why they say the things they say. This exploration is usually well received. Patients recognize that they have goals that are not conscious.

After exploring what they need when opening up, a wide range of motivations emerge. Common responses include:

"I don't know."

"I guess I wanted help but didn't want to acknowledge it."

"I give advice because I feel uncomfortable."

"I want attention."

"I want to be included."

"I was anxious in the silence."

I frequently add that sometimes we just want a witness. Patients have come back to group reporting that they found reflecting on why they were saying what they were saying was a very uncomfortable experience. Some members felt it interfered with their spontaneity. I would ask them if spontaneity was more important than being understood.

They recognized how they were communicating without giving much thought to what they were saying or considering the effect it was having on the person they were relating to. Over time, many patients would report that the self-reflection and awareness of their goals in communication, even though uncomfortable, was very helpful in becoming more effective in communicating what they wanted to say. Some volunteered that they actually felt less awkward in interpersonal moments.

Witnessing in Group

I use certain expressions that patients report being helpful in recognizing what their purpose is when communicating in group. Needing someone to be a witness has been one of those frames that patients say they never thought of. They often respond that it resonates very well with what they were hoping for in an interpersonal moment.

Erica, a relatively new member of the group, brought up that she often had a problem with her husband. When bringing up something that was bothering her, he would inevitably give her advice that she would promptly reject. This usually led to an outcome that would alternate between mutual frustration or ending up in a fight, with him saying, "I don't know what you want from me." Her husband would complain that she "always rejected what he had to say." She would respond that what he had to say was "dumb."

Following a group meeting where she discovered that sometimes we just want or need a witness, she prefaced an interaction with her husband, clarifying that what she needed was "for you to be my witness." He responded with "So you just want me to listen?" She answered, "Yes, I'd like you to listen, but also I want you to be my witness." He finally got it.

She was very grateful to the group for contributing to the change in how she related to her husband. She shared with the group, "Now I finally realize why you're always saying we should explore our 'nickel in the dime.' I had no idea that I was contributing to the problem that came up so often with my husband."

Defensive Styles in Group

While facilitating groups, I have come across many creative defensive styles. Some defenses are quite obvious to me, others are not. Some relatively obvious defenses are patients looking at the floor, gazing out the window, not looking at the person they are speaking to, arriving to group chronically late, talking over someone, etc. (Ormont, 1992).

Some defensive styles that are less obvious are:

1. One defensive style can be called the polite, "as if" defense or, as my patient Karen defined it, her "Southern Charm" defense.

    This occurs when the patient appears to be participating, cooperating, and engaging but is actually not letting themselves be affected by who or what they are engaging in. They are actually attempting to control the process in the group by appearing falsely compliant, responsive, and agreeable.

    This defensive style was evident when Karen, after being in the group for two years, cheerfully let the group know that this was going to be her last group. She just got a position that would take much more of her time and didn't want to "shortchange" the group. She made it appear that she was doing a service for the group. She didn't wait for anyone to say anything before launching into, "So how do I do this?"

Without hesitation, she answered her own question. "I guess I can say goodbye to everyone individually and tell them how much they mean to me." Then without skipping a beat, smiling a big smile, she started telling Riley, one of her groupmates, how much she appreciated her directness and authenticity.

I asked Riley what her experience was like as she was being validated by Karen. Her response was, "I'm reluctant to say this because Karen is being so gracious, but I don't buy it. I feel I'm being charmed into going along with a charade."

I asked Karen what her reaction was to hearing this. Her response was, "I guess I'm busted. I was using my Southern Charm to try to get through this difficult moment. My family members were masters at this."

2.   Another defensive style, used by my patient Pam, was labeled the "ask a lot of questions" defense.

At first, Pam's questions seemed helpful in clarifying what another member was revealing.

After several more questions, I asked the group what their experience was like listening to all the questions Pam was asking. Responses varied from being bored to feeling impatient with Pam.

I asked Pam what her experience was like below all the questions. She revealed that it was a way to interact with her family while keeping them at arm's length and not "get clobbered."

3.   Noah regularly would challenge something I would say, using what we called his "debate defense."

Noah was a therapist and would use his knowledge and experience to say that I wasn't seeing something (which may have been true), I was on the wrong track, I didn't take something into account, etc. His tone seemed elevated and judgmental. At certain points I would find myself debating him. I asked the group if they recognized a pattern developing between Noah and me. Several commented on how it seemed I would let myself get into a debate with Noah instead of maintaining my usual stance of exploring his reactions. I realized it was true.

The debate defense seemed to pull me into a role lock with Noah. When I asked him what his experience was like when he was debating with me, he was surprised to remember that he would debate his harsh and judgmental father when he wanted his attention. His father, a professor of law at a renowned university, seemed to find special time for Noah when Noah could find a topic that would provoke his father into a debate.

Noah acknowledged that his debating me left him initially feeling excited and energized. Ultimately, he would feel the experience to be frustrating and disappointing. This pattern was not unfamiliar to him. His wife would complain that "simple, easy-going discussions" would end up becoming an unpleasant battle of wills about minor unimportant points. He never realized the meaning it had. He now realized it was not resulting in the attention that he unconsciously desired. It actually led to his undermining the closeness he was hoping for.

4. Alice would often respond to questions or comments directed to her with responses that were *tangential* to what was being said. After several instances of her groupmates pointing out this pattern, she suddenly exclaimed, "I'm just distracted."

I asked Alice to reflect on what her experience was like when she was "just distracted." After exploring for a moment, she recognized that her tangential response was a subtle attempt on her part to respond without really responding. She did not want to reveal herself. She shared that she developed this pattern in her family of origin to avoid getting into a battle of wills with her mother after witnessing the difficulties her sister had in being honest with Mom. She remembered being seen in her family as "a scatterbrain." Whenever Alice would respond in a way that seemed obtuse or tangential, someone in the group would sooner or later suggest that it seemed that she was going into her "just distracted" or "scatterbrain defense."

These are some of the many defensive patterns that have emerged in my groups over time. Recognizing them has helped me establish mutual assumptions about how these patterns of behavior can be understood to be a security system or solution for the patient that was originally developed in response to stressful situations in their family of origin.

Recognizing and naming these patterns as a *defense* has helped group members recognize what their "nickel in the dime" is when they find themselves in interpersonal difficulties. These defenses, or solutions, no longer work as well as they once did and are anachronisms that are generally dysfunctional in the current context of the patient's life.

Process vs. Content

In facilitating groups over the years, I have witnessed and experienced how important it is to differentiate *process* from *content*. I have learned that sometimes content should stay at the forefront of the group experience; sometimes process should be the focus. They are both always present. It is up to me, the therapist, to help the group focus on one or the other, depending on the needs of the moment (Yalom & Leszcz, 2005). At certain times, we need content to give us context as to what a member is working on in the group as well as outside of the group.

The group should know important identifying features of everyone in the group. Group members should be familiar with each member's profession or job, intimate relationships, family structure, presenting complaints as to what they are working on in group, etc. Sometimes important content is overlooked, bypassed, or forgotten as the group focuses on the process of the group.

I have been a member of groups, have facilitated groups, and have supervised therapists where the group energy has been so focused on the here-and-now process of the group that over time members had little idea of what their groupmates' lives were like outside of group. When this occurs, I always attempt to explore the process of why this is happening. Sometimes members would not report on important changes in their lives. They would not report or recognize how the group was helping or not helping them with these changes.

In some groups that appeared to be working well, I've noticed patients often have no idea what they are working on in the group. They also do not know what their groupmates are working on in the group experience.

The "Don't Ask, Don't Tell" Group

My focus in group is generally process over content. I am continually facilitating the exploration of patients' experiences in group. It is too easy for patients to hide behind content, behind storytelling. However, I have also seen the opposite. I have experienced group processes where, over time, members are so focused on process that they avoid connecting it to the content and context of their lives outside the group. These groups seem to use process to defend against acknowledging or revealing important content. They appear active in the here-and-now process of the group, but they avoid reporting important issues in their outside lives.

This often happens when patients have gotten a handle on some of the problems that led them to therapy in the first place. In general, those issues morph into other challenges that emerge in the group.

> Mark entered therapy because he wanted help in "changing his wife." He came into therapy believing it would provide him with the tools to achieve that goal. He was surprised and disappointed to learn that we can't change anyone.
>
> He became interested in the prospect of using group to learn how to affect another person. He was very available to discovering his "nickel in the dime."

He was very open to paying attention to how he was affecting others in group, which gave him some idea how he might be affecting others in his life.

Gradually, Mark reported that positive changes were happening in his marriage. He reported listening more attentively, being more curious about why his wife said what she said, instead of debating her. He began to voice his needs more clearly instead of expecting his wife to read his mind. The tension in his marriage was greatly reduced. He credited the group experience for helping with the changes.

Mark, over the next few years, continued to be an active member in the process of the group. He was satisfied that the group was working for him and used the group to hone his interpersonal skills. However, he stopped bringing in significant challenges in his life. He never mentioned that he was feeling worn out, dissatisfied at work, and was having trouble with his boss.

He did not reveal that he had been losing significant amounts of money gambling on stocks even though the market kept going up. Mark noticed that members would not update each other on what was happening in their outside lives and decided to do the same. Over time, Mark's group, which stayed in the process of the here and now so skillfully, seemed to have gradually developed a group-as-a-whole avoidance in not bringing in material issues that were troubling them in their lives outside of the group.

I brought this up at some point, and several long-term members revealed that they wanted to keep the group isolated as a safe haven that didn't include problems that they were having in their outside life. One member revealed that he didn't want to "open up another can of worms." I asked why group could not be both a safe haven and an opportunity to work on issues they were currently struggling with in their lives.

I hypothesized that the group, where members appeared to be engaged, had developed a subtle "as if" defense that paralleled many members' intimate relationships. I facilitated the exploration of the experience of group members being in what one member labeled a "don't ask, don't tell" group.

I pointed out that it seemed that members rarely revealed what was going on in their outside lives. I also pointed out what appeared to be a process of members having entered into a silent agreement not to ask each other about their outside lives. This exploration resulted in a flood of content. The group seemed to come alive.

I understood this to be an example of a Basic Assumption group in flight that was not obvious. Members appeared to be engaging each other in the group process while withholding— consciously and unconsciously—content that was material to what they were working on, or should have been working on, in their therapy.

Group Member Bolts Out of the Session

Over the years, on rare occasions, a flare-up occurs when a member stands up and physically leaves the group. Having been a participant in groups where this would happen, I noted that the facilitator would let the patient leave the meeting. He would then process the experience with the remaining group members. Frequently, the group member would not return. Sometimes they would quit. If they did return, the group would process the experience of the enactment and the group would move on. When this has happened in groups I lead, I have experienced very positive outcomes in asking the group to continue to work while I leave the office and attempt to talk to the patient who bolted out of the room.

I would catch up with the member, who inevitably had to wait for the elevator. I would make an effort to gently encourage the patient to return to the group meeting and work through what just happened. More often than not, the patient would return to the session. In some cases, the patient would say they were too upset and thought they should just go home. I would support either decision. If the member didn't return until the next meeting, I would explore, with the group, their experience of what just happened.

When the member returned for the next session, group members would generally unpack their experience of what occurred. During this exploration I would make it a point to ask the patient who left the session what their experience was like when I went out of the office to talk to them. The general response was gratitude for not being shamed and left alone.

Other members' responses ranged from, "If that happened in my family, my parents would just let me leave, stew in my anger, and ultimately shame me," to being grateful that "if that happened to me, it is comforting to know that you wouldn't just leave me alone in the extreme discomfort of what I did." Frequently, the patient would comment that it helped them return to the group.

Tendencies to Blame and Complain

Two useful phrases I use in responding to patients who complain and blame:

1. "Our goal is to make the relationship with the world you can make, giving up the relationship with the world you want."

   I understand this notion to be Yvonne Agazarian's (1997) clarification that to get to our goals we have no choice but to deal with the frustrations of reality.

2. "The entitled fantasy of finding a receptive container."

   Billow (2000), in recounting Bion's work, uses this phrase to address patients' complaints about how they are being treated by others or the world in general. It is our responsibility to relate effectively in our interactions with others. It is up to us to attempt to achieve the relationships that we want. We are not entitled to have others relate to us in the way we would like or believe we deserve. The world is not our receptive container.

Addressing Nonverbal Provocations

Frequently, patients will have a particular tone in their voice that reveals an emotion that is not acknowledged or even recognized by them. It is so much part of a person's experience they do not realize the effect it is having on the other person (Ormont, 1992). It frequently is ego-syntonic.

Generally, this tone communicates anger, frustration, judgment, disbelief, upset, etc. It can also communicate attraction, desire, friendliness, love, etc. When it is pointed out, aggressive emotion is often denied. Provocative and inadvertently seductive emotion is often not recognized.

These indirect expressions of emotion commonly provoke uncomfortable responses in others. The patient is generally unaware that they are communicating in ways that could be experienced as aggressive, provocative, seductive, controlling, etc. I regularly point out a patient's nonverbal communication during the group process. I draw attention to how the tone, language, volume, etc., of their communication is affecting others.

The next step, of course, is to help the patient recognize the experience that was obscured by the nonverbal communication. My goal is to help patients pay attention to how they are communicating in order to find unambiguous, effective language that expresses what the patient is experiencing and intends to say.

Using the Patient's Words

In my training, one very helpful recommendation was to use the patient's words in exploring whatever they were bringing into the session. I have found that exploring the connotation of actual words leads me to more fully understand the meaning these words have for a particular patient. This fine tuning has helped me to better understand my patient's experience, as well as how they understand their experience.

When a patient expresses experiences such as "I feel [or don't feel] understood, safe, related to, alone, despairing, depressed," I use the patient's actual language in my attempt to make certain I understand what their words mean to *them*, not what *I* think they mean.

For example, patients use the word *depression* to describe many different states of mind and being. I always follow up on how they are using the term. I will inquire, using their words, "What's your experience when you say you feel depressed, immobilized, bored, sad, hopeless, etc.?" Clarifying what the group member means when they are using specific language helps me better understand and become more empathically attuned to that particular individual.

Using the patient's exact words also serves as a model for group members in general, who tend to make assumptions about what their groupmates mean when relating to each other. They are often mistaken.

Chapter 17

Endings

Reframing "We're Going Around in Circles"

Occasionally, patients will complain about their group experience, suggesting that the group "is going around in circles." In exploring what their experience is below the complaint, these patients will protest that the topics that we explore come up "over and over again." I generally respond that in group we don't discuss "topics." We are attempting to explore what our emotional experience is below the content we are focused on.

The response generally is, yes, they understand that, but it seems, "we're just going around in circles."

During one of these explorations, Lou, an advertising exec who would often come up with very insightful and timely observations, brought up his experience related to going over the same stuff in group. He suggested,

> Yes, we do go over the same things, over and over again. However, my experience is that we're climbing a mountain together. As we climb around the mountain, we do, of course, see the same scenery and views over and over again. The difference for me is that each time we circle the mountain, we're gradually going up the mountain. As we go up the mountain, our perspective of the same views and vistas changes because we're looking at them from a higher angle. I realize that as we go up our mountain, the group issues are the same, but our perspective related to them changes. The same north, south, east, and west views that we inevitably will see evolve as our perspective changes while we make our way to our goals.

The Process of Termination

Inevitably, at some point, we are all going to face the experience of leaving the group. Most patients will end having had a successful therapeutic experience, some will not. Therapists leaving or disbanding a group and patients leaving a group inevitably have experiences related to ending and loss that are

DOI: 10.4324/9781003649632-17

difficult to face and are frequently avoided by an abortive ending (Yalom & Leszcz, 2005).

I have found the process of termination to be very challenging but rewarding for all members of the group, as well as the group leader (Ormont, 1992). I believe it is very meaningful for members in the group to experience the loss of the terminating member as a death. I ask my patients not to have contact with the member who is leaving in the same way I ask them not to have contact with each other while they are in group.

Frequently, members protest my suggestion not to have contact after the terminating member leaves. When we explore below the protest, we frequently find that members do not want to face the reality of the ending of very significant relationships in their lives.

Some patients do not want to admit the full extent of feelings they have toward the terminating patient. Some patients have difficulty saying out loud how much the group meant to them. Sometimes patients want to avoid the thought that they did not have much impact on others in the group. Some patients find it much too difficult to truly say goodbye. Others have difficulty with the feelings that emerge around the true finality of death. They admit that they can intellectually acknowledge the reality of death but find it overwhelming to experience in the moment.

When patients bring up their desire to end group therapy, I always try to explore their decision in a supportive manner. I try to help them articulate their motivations in leaving and understand what their leaving means to them and the group. After taking time to explore a patient's desire to leave group, I suggest that they go through the process of termination. I tell them that this will give everyone a chance to digest their decision as well as be a way to say goodbye. In general, I suggest that termination should last about four sessions. Sometimes the termination lasts longer when unresolved issues emerge. At times the patient is unwilling to stay even for the four sessions I recommend.

During the termination process, I ask patients to reflect on the goals they have accomplished as well as the issues they still have to work on. I ask them to reflect on the group experience. What worked for them? What did not? What will they miss? What did they learn about themselves that was important to them?

If the member leaving feels that the group experience was not helpful in some way, I ask them what they plan to do in order to seek the help they need. I also suggest that they should not hesitate to contact me for a referral if they are open to it.

The process of termination is often a time when members express emotion that may not have been previously revealed. I have seen members in some instances open up a wide range of emotion, from previously unexpressed affection to split-off anger and upset.

On occasion, I have had the experience of observing groups and group leaders making it very difficult for a patient to leave. We can always find reasons why the patient should stay. We can always find issues that still can be worked on. When this occurs in a group that I am facilitating, after exploring the patient's desire to leave, I make it a point to respectfully support their decision. I then explore the sentiment that is subtly or not so subtly being conveyed in the group.

"Is there a subtle communication in group suggesting that Ava stay in group even if it isn't working for her? Is the group reluctant to let Ava leave without subtly inducing guilt or doubt in her? Several members keep bringing up that Ava still has work to do. Is this group the only place where Ava can work on these issues?"

After exploring a patient's decision to leave the group, I always make it a point to support the patient, regardless of whether I think they should stay or not. Termination can also be a rich opportunity for the group to explore their experience of a patient's leaving group.

As the group explored their experience of Ava's leaving, responses ranged from, "We failed her" to "I'm afraid the group is going to fail me too" to "Good riddance." We continued to explore all these responses before and after Ava left the group. These explorations opened up a wealth of personal experiences and projections focused on fear, trust, and dependency that was being acted out in the group's response to Ava's leaving.

Most terminations that I have been a part of have been a time for reflection, appreciation, and sometimes disappointment. Members tend to recount the time spent together working on issues that were never revealed in any other place or to any other person.

It's All Grist for the Mill

Over the years, I've come across many sage aphorisms that say a lot with very little. The sentiment in the expression "It's all grist for the mill" has been invaluable in clarifying the underlying way I approach group therapy

In my practice as a group therapist, I have found all our experiences in the group process, good and bad, comfortable and uncomfortable, safe and unsafe, to be essential in developing a path to discovering what holds us back from bringing out the best in ourselves and ultimately finding a way to reach our goals. It's all grist for the mill.

References

Agazarian, Y. M. (1997). *Systems-centered therapy for groups.* Guilford Press.

Alcoholics Anonymous. (2001). *Alcoholics Anonymous: The story of how many thousands of men and women have recovered from alcoholism* (4th ed.). Alcoholics Anonymous World Services.

American Psychiatric Association. (2013). *Diagnostic and statistical manual of mental disorders: DSM-5^{TM}* (5th ed.). American Psychiatric Publishing.

Bacal, H. A. (1985). Object-relations in the group from the perspective of self psychology. *International Journal of Group Psychotherapy*, 35(4), 483–501.

Billow, R. M. (2000). Relational levels of the "container–contained" in group therapy. *Group*, 24(3), 243–259.

Festinger, L. (1957). *A theory of cognitive dissonance.* Stanford University Press.

Frankl, V. E. (2006). *Man's search for meaning* (I. Lasch, Trans.). Beacon Press.

Gabbard, G. O. (1994). *Psychodynamic psychiatry in clinical practice* (2nd ed.). American Psychiatric Press.

Gorkin, M. (1987). *The uses of countertransference.* Jason Aronson.

Greenberg, J. R., & Mitchell, S. A. (1983). *Object relations in psychoanalytic theory.* Harvard University Press.

Greenson, R. R. (1967). *The technique and practice of psychoanalysis.* International Universities Press.

Hendrix, H. (2007). *Getting the love you want: A guide for couples* (20th Anniversary ed.). Henry Holt.

Kernberg, O. F. (1975). *Borderline conditions and pathological narcissism.* Jason Aronson.

Kibel, H. D. (1993). Object relations theory and group psychotherapy. In H. I. Kaplan, & B. J. Sadock (Eds.), *Comprehensive group psychotherapy* (3rd ed.). Lippincott Williams and Wilkins, pp. 165–176.

Mahler, M. S., Pine, F., & Bergman, A. (1975). *The psychological birth of the human infant.* Basic Books.

McWilliams, N. (1984). *Psychoanalytic diagnosis: Understanding personality structure in the clinical process.* Guilford Press.

Miller, A. (1997). *The drama of the gifted child: The search for the true self* (3rd ed.). Basic Books.

Mitchell, S. A., & Black, M. (1995). *Freud and beyond: A history of modern psychoanalytic thought.* Basic Books.

Ormont, L. (1992). *The group therapy experience*. St. Martin's Press.

Rutan, J. S., & Stone, W. N. (2001). *Psychodynamic group psychotherapy* (3rd ed.). Guilford Press.

Tansey, M. J., & Burke, W. F. (1989). *Understanding countertransference: From projective identification to empathy*. Analytic Press.

Winnicott, D. W. (1971). *Playing and reality*. Penguin.

Wright, F. (2000). The use of the self in group leadership: A relational perspective. *International Journal of Group Psychotherapy*, 50, 181–198.

Yalom, I. D., & Leszcz, M. (2005). *The theory and practice of group psychotherapy* (5th ed.). Basic Books.

Index

For Product Safety Concerns and Information please contact our EU
representative GPSR@taylorandfrancis.com
Taylor & Francis Verlag GmbH, Kaufingerstraße 24, 80331 München, Germany

www.ingramcontent.com/pod-product-compliance
Lightning Source LLC
Chambersburg PA
CBHW050613280326
41932CB00016B/3021